Nicolas de Clamanges

CHRISTOPHER M. BELLITTO

Nicolas de Clamanges

Spirituality, Personal Reform,
and Pastoral Renewal on the
Eve of the Reformations

The Catholic University of America Press
Washington, D.C.

The paper used in this publication meets the minimum requirements of
American National Standards for Information Science—Permanence of
Paper for Printed Library materials, ANSI Z39.48-1984.

Library of Congress Cataloging-in-Publication Data

Bellitto, Christopher M.

Nicolas de Clamanges: spirituality, personal reform, and pastoral
renewal on the eve of the reformations / Christopher M. Bellitto.

p. cm.

Includes bibliographical references and index.

1. Clamanges, Nicolas de, 1363 or 4–1437. I. Title.

BX 4705.C57 B45   2001

282'.092-dc21

00-030311

ISBN 0-8132-0996-x (alk. paper)

for Karen,
my wife and my best friend,
who believes in me

Contents

❧ ☙

Acknowledgments

❦❦

No book is the fruit of the author's efforts alone. My thanks go to the following who provided advice, materials, and encouragement: François Bérier, Alan Bernstein, Dario Cecchetti, Gerald Christianson, Francis Corry, Lawrence Hundersmarck, Thomas Izbicki, Daniel LaCorte, Chris Nighman, Joseph O'Callaghan, Gilbert Ouy, Steven Spishak. The library staffs at Fordham University, St. Joseph's Seminary, and the New York Public Library provided much assistance, as did the members of the Interlibrary Loan system. David McGonagle, Susan Needham, and Elizabeth Kerr of the Catholic University of America Press guided this project with steady, professional hands. I have expanded here my article, "The Spirituality of Reform in the Late Medieval Church: The Example of Nicolas de Clamanges," *Church History* 68 (1999): 1–13, © 1999, The American Society of Church History. I am particularly indebted to Phillip Stump, who read the manuscript several times and offered insightful recommendations. I especially thank Louis B. Pascoe, S.J., who guided my doctoral studies in the rigid academic tradition of Gerhart Ladner and the affirming *cura personalis* of Ignatius Loyola. The word "mentor" is overused. Fr. Pascoe is among the very few who deserve the honor of that title.

Ad maiorem Dei gloriam
C. M. B.

Abbreviations

❧❧

B [followed by volume, page, and line numbers]
François Bérier, ed. "Nicolas de Clamanges. Opuscules." 2 vols.
Ph.D. diss., École Pratique de Hautes Études, 1974.

Bernstein, NP
Alan E. Bernstein. "Nicholas Poillevillain of Clamanges: A
Critical Biography Presented with an Annotated Bibliography of
His Published Works." Typescript, Columbia University, 1968.

C [followed by page and line numbers]
Dario Cecchetti, ed. "L'epistolario di Nicolas de Clamanges."
Ph.D. diss., Università degli Studi di Torino, 1960.

CC
Corpus Christianorum

CIC
E. Friedberg, ed. *Corpus Iuris Canonici.* 2 vols. Leipzig: Bernhard
Tauchnitz, 1879–81.

Coville, *Recherches*
Alfred Coville. *Recherches sur quelques écrivains du XIVe et du
XVe siècle.* Paris: Droz, 1935.

Coville, *Le Traité*
Alfred Coville. *Le Traité de la ruine de l'Église de Nicholas de
Clamanges et la traduction française de 1564.* Paris: Droz, 1936.

CSEL
Corpus Scriptorum Ecclesiasticorum Latinorum

d'Achery
Luc d'Achery, ed. *Spicilegium sive collectio veterum aliquot scriptorum qui in Galliae bibliothecis delituerant.* 13 vols. Paris, 1655–77.

L [followed by volume and page numbers]
J. Lydius, ed. *Nicolai de Clemangiis. Opera Omnia.* 3 vols. Leiden, 1613. Reprint in one volume, Farnborough, Hants., England: Gregg Press Limited, 1967.

Ladner, *The Idea of Reform*
Gerhart B. Ladner. *The Idea of Reform: Its Impact on Christian Thought and Action in the Age of the Fathers.* Cambridge: Harvard University Press, 1959. Reprint, New York: Harper & Row, 1967.

Ornato, *Jean Muret*
Ezio Ornato. *Jean Muret et ses amis, Nicolas de Clamanges et Jean de Montreuil. Contribution à l'étude des rapports entre les humanistes de Paris et ceux d'Avignon (1394–1420).* Geneva: Droz, 1969.

Pascoe, *Jean Gerson*
Louis B. Pascoe. *Jean Gerson: Principles of Church Reform.* Leiden: E. J. Brill, 1973.

PL
J.-P. Migne, ed. Patrologia Latina.

Stump, *Reforms*
Phillip H. Stump. *The Reforms of the Council of Constance (1414–1418).* Leiden: E. J. Brill, 1994.

Nicolas de Clamanges

Introduction

❦

The name Nicolas de Clamanges (1363/64–1437) is well known, but Clamanges as a religious reformer has been unjustly neglected and substantially overlooked. He was involved in the resolution of the Great Schism, the beginnings of French humanism, the internal and external politics of the University of Paris and the French royal family, and reform in the late medieval Church. The efforts of his mentor Pierre d'Ailly (1350–1420) and his classmate Jean Gerson (1363–1429) have outshone Clamanges' role in reform. Furthermore, his writings were declared to be suspect after his death, and he was cursorily labeled as a proto-Protestant reformer: some or all of his works variously appeared on the *Index Librorum Prohibitorum* from 1549 to 1897.[1] What scholarly attention Clamanges has attracted is relatively recent and focuses primarily on the literary, humanistic elements of his writings as opposed to their religious characteristics. In his lifetime, as well, he first attracted notice through his linguistic virtuosity. Clamanges was *rédacteur* of the University of Paris and drafted the academic community's official correspondence. He later served twice as secretary to the Avignon pope Benedict XIII (1394–1417). As a result, for his time and ours Clamanges' own stylish pen overshadows the equally important aspects of religious reform found in his writings. Since only half the story of Nicolas de Clamanges has been told, the present study hopes to redress the balance. Clamanges was far more than an elegant writer. He was a religious reformer who turned his attention to the renewal of the late medieval Church as frequently as he emulated classical literature. Although he did not attain the recognition or dominant influence of d'Ailly and Gerson, Clamanges still played an important role in Church reform. By choice and circumstance he preferred to work for the reform of the Church far from the centers of

---

1. Alfred Coville, "Nicolas de Clamanges à l'Index au XVIe siècle," in *Mélanges offerts à M. Abel Lefranc* (Paris: Droz, 1936), 1–16.

power and influence. He spent about twenty years in two active exiles in French monasteries and countryside retreats writing reform treatises and letters to influential prelates, scholars, and royal officials. This considerable *opus* indicates that he was working intently, albeit in a self-assigned role as a backstage exhorter rather than as a powerful negotiator, to unite and reform the late medieval Church.

Clamanges' life and thought were interwoven with the events of his day, and so it is important to begin this study of his slighted contributions to religious reform with a detailed review of the Schism and the many attempts to reform the Church in head and members. We shall see that within this context Clamanges frequently built his reform ideas on biblical, patristic, and humanistic principles. With rhetorical flair, he advocated a foundational *reformatio personalis,* a personal path to reform that must be presupposed if the Church *in capite et in membris* was to be reformed in a lasting and meaningful way. Relying on the activist spirituality of the late Middle Ages, especially the *imitatio Christi* devotions, Clamanges identified the personal path to reform as a *via purgativa* that would temper the soul and pave the way toward heaven. Clamanges' plans for personal reform did not end with the individual; they moved forward into a broader program of Church reform. Personal reform, though key and indispensable, was the means to the greater goal of reforming pastoral care within the Church. He built outwards from the interior core of a *reformatio personalis* to consider its next logical progression: the improvement of pastoral care and service through the institutional reform of the Church. His criticisms of simony, hypocrisy, failures in the *cura animarum,* and the irrelevancy of late medieval scholastic education were all ultimately aimed at reemphasizing the fact that the primary task of pope, bishop, and priest was to shepherd God's flock.

Reformatio personalis was the fulcrum around which Clamanges' reform thought turned and the characteristic that distinguishes him. The centrality of *reformatio personalis* is especially seen in his comments on the individual spiritual progress and scholastic training of the prospective cleric charged with the *cura animarum in membris.* These foreshadowed Trent more than they anticipated Luther. Once he had set his own spiritual house in order, the personally reformed and pastorally oriented shepherd could then aid the *reformatio personalis* of his flock. In this focus Clamanges conveyed to the late Middle Ages the seminal concern of patristic reform: the personal, individual reform of Christian believers as opposed to the institutional reform of the *Ecclesia,* a concept that did not enter the mainstream of reform thought until the Gregorian Revolution began in the eleventh century.

It should be noted that Clamanges was not entirely unique in the attention he paid to *reformatio personalis* and reform *in membris.* But what sets him apart is the key role he assigned to *reformatio personalis* in late medieval reform thought. Clamanges placed *reformatio personalis* squarely at the center of his ideas: personal reform was the *sine qua non* for the renewal of the late medieval Church. Other reformers, by contrast, saw personal reform as the product of institutional reform *in capite* that would trickle down through the body of the Church. Gerson described personal reform as the result of hierarchical reform that properly began *in capite.* As Louis B. Pascoe put it in his study of the principles of Gerson's reform thought, "All ecclesiastical reform must, in the final analysis, terminate in personal reform if it is to be in any way effective." Delegates at Constance envisioned reform *in capite* "as a vital prerequisite to the reform of the members; according to the prevailing hierarchical view reform would extend down from the head to the members," as Phillip H. Stump assesses the matter in his recent reappraisal of reform at Constance.[2]

Clamanges' religious ideas have been almost entirely ignored by modern scholars, so we aim here to introduce, illustrate, and analyze his reform thought in its theory and application. We hope to locate Clamanges' position among the ranks of reformers working during the Schism and to focus increased attention on this aspect of his thought. Given these purposes, it is important to place this study within the current state of research on Church reform, a topic whose popularity is tied

---

2. Pascoe, *Jean Gerson,* 175. Stump, *Reforms,* 138; see also 169: ". . . the truth is that the conciliar reformers themselves placed their first emphasis on reform *in capite.* They did so, however, because they believed that it was the most urgent and would in turn make possible true reform *in membris,* to be enacted at future councils which would meet regularly according to the decree *Frequens.*"

to the rising interest in Church reform of our own times as ushered in by the deliberations of the Second Vatican Council.[3] Clamanges' reform principles and plans will be explicated and analyzed according to the methodology of Gerhart B. Ladner who pioneered the ideological approach to the study of Church reform just before Vatican II in *The Idea of Reform: Its Impact on Christian Thought and Action in the Age of the Fathers.*[4] Ladner's methodology stresses textual and contextual analysis of the idea of reform in its diverse formulations and the manner in which these formulations influenced the construction of concrete programs of reform. Ladner studied the theory and imagery of reform in the patristic, early medieval, and high medieval periods. This study adds to Ladner's foundation as part of a second generation of reform studies, which have moved his categories forward to trace their developments and applications in the late medieval, Renaissance, and Reformation periods.[5]

Scholars have largely overlooked Clamanges' reform thought, yet they have not entirely ignored him. His name briefly appears in standard

3. Historical studies of reform done in the context of Vatican II include Y.-M. Congar, *Vraie et fausse réforme dans l'Église,* 2d ed. (Paris: Les Éditions du Cerf, 1968); Robert E. McNally, *Reform of the Church* (New York: Herder and Herder, 1963) and *The Unreformed Church* (New York: Sheed and Ward, 1965); and John W. O'Malley, "Reform, Historical Consciousness, and Vatican II's *Aggiornamento,*" *Theological Studies* 32 (1971): 573–601.

4. *The Idea of Reform* was first published by Harvard University Press in 1959 and then reprinted by Harper & Row in 1967. Ladner's articles are collected in *Images and Ideas in the Middle Ages* (Rome: Edizioni di Storia e Letteratura, 1983). For a discussion of Ladner's contributions and a complete bibliography, see John Van Engen, "Images and Ideas: The Achievements of Gerhart Burian Ladner, with a Bibliography of His Published Works," *Viator* 20 (1989): 85–115.

5. Among Ladner's students see Pascoe, *Jean Gerson,* "Jean Gerson: Mysticism, Conciliarism, and Reform," *Annuarium historiae conciliorum* 6 (1974): 135–53, "Jean Gerson: The *Ecclesia primitiva* and Reform," *Traditio* 30 (1974): 379–409, and "Theological Dimensions of Pierre d'Ailly's Teaching on Papal Plenitude of Power," *Annuarium historiae conciliorum* 11 (1979): 357–66; Van Engen, *Rupert of Deutz* (Berkeley: University of California Press, 1983); and Stump, *Reforms.* Among others see O'Malley, "Historical Thought and the Reform Crisis of the Early Sixteenth Century," *Theological Studies* 28 (1967): 531–48, *Giles of Viterbo on Church and Reform: A Study in Renaissance Thought* (Leiden: E. J. Brill, 1968), and *Praise and Blame in Renaissance Rome: Rhetoric, Doctrine and Reform in the Sacred Orators of the Papal Court, c. 1450–1521* (Durham, N.C.: Duke University Press, 1979); McNally, "The Council of Trent, the Spiritual Exercises and the Catholic Reform," *Church History* 34 (1965): 36–49, and "Pope Adrian VI (1522–23) and Church Reform," *Archivum historiae pontificiae* 7 (1969): 253–85; and Nelson H. Minnich, "Concepts of Reform Proposed at the Fifth Lateran Council," *Archivum historiae pontificiae* 7 (1969): 163–251.

histories of the late medieval Church and the Schism. Clamanges is considered in particular studies of his close friends, as in Francis Oakley's treatment of d'Ailly's political thought or in Pascoe's examination of the reform principles of Gerson.[6] A chronological accounting of Clamanges' life may be discovered in an unpublished Columbia University seminar paper by Alan E. Bernstein and a monograph by Ezio Ornato on the humanists in Clamanges' circle of friends.[7] Most of the attention paid to Clamanges stems from his deep learning in the classics. He has been studied as an early French humanist, as in several monographs by Alfred Coville.[8] More recent works of a similar focus have been produced exclusively by European scholars, primarily Gilbert Ouy[9] and Dario Cecchet-

6. References to Gerson eclipse those to Clamanges in Francis Oakley, *The Political Thought of Pierre d'Ailly: The Voluntarist Tradition* (New Haven: Yale University Press, 1964), and in the biographical portrait of d'Ailly in Bernard Guenée, *Between Church and State: The Lives of Four French Prelates in the Late Middle Ages,* trans. Arthur Goldhammer (Chicago: University of Chicago Press, 1991), 102–258. Similarly, D. Catherine Brown discusses d'Ailly much more often than she does Clamanges in *Pastor and Laity in the Theology of Jean Gerson* (Cambridge: Cambridge University Press, 1987). Pascoe refers more frequently to d'Ailly than Clamanges in his *Jean Gerson.* Most strikingly, d'Ailly is often present while Clamanges appears only in a single footnote in Mark S. Burrows, *Jean Gerson and De Consolatione Theologiae (1418): The Consolation of a Biblical and Reforming Theology for a Disordered Age* (Tübingen: J. C. B. Mohr [Paul Siebeck], 1991). Clamanges was not even included in an important study of the University of Paris by R. N. Swanson, *Universities, Academics and the Great Schism* (Cambridge: Cambridge University Press, 1979).

7. Bernstein, NP, and Ornato, *Jean Muret*; my thanks to Dr. Bernstein for supplying a copy of his paper. Anton Simon's dissertation from Albert-Ludwigs-Universität provided a summary of Clamanges' life and identified his concerns with humanism, politics, and religious reform and unity: *Studien zu Nikolaus von Clemanges* (Endingen: Druck von Emil Wild, 1929).

8. Alfred Coville, *Gontier et Pierre Col et l'humanisme en France au temps de Charles VI* (Paris: Droz, 1934), *Recherches sur quelques écrivains du XIVe et du XVe siècle* (Paris: Droz, 1935), and *La vie intellectuelle dans les domaines d'Avignon-Provence, de 1380 à 1435* (Paris: Droz, 1941).

9. Gilbert Ouy, "Paris, l'un des principaux foyers de l'humanisme en Europe au début du XVe siècle," *Bulletin de la société de l'histoire de Paris et de l'Île-de-France* (1967–68): 71–98; "Le thème du 'Taedium scriptorum gentilium' chez les humanistes, particulièrement en France au début du XVe siècle," *Cahiers de l'association internationale des études française* 23 (1971): 9–26; "Le collège de Navarre, berceau de l'humanisme français," *Actes du 95e congrès national des sociétés savantes, Reims 1970. Section de philologie et d'histoire jusqu'à 1610,* vol. 1, *Enseignement et vie intellectuelle (IXe–XVIe siècle)* (Paris: Bibliothèque Nationale, 1975), 275–99; and "In Search of the Earliest Traces of French Humanism: The Evidence from Codicology," *Library Chronicle* 43 (1978): 3–38.

ti.[10] All of these studies have principally been humanistic, linguistic, and codicological analyses, although François Bérier has more recently directed attention toward the religious and political content of Clamanges' texts.[11]

Despite the interest Clamanges' writings have raised concerning his literary style and content, a modern critical edition of his complete works remains a *desideratum*. He wrote fourteen treatises of widely varying lengths, about one hundred and fifty letters, and about a dozen prayers and poems. The oldest, almost complete printed collection of Clamanges' works was compiled in three volumes by J. Lydius in 1613. Lydius, as subsequent editors of Clamanges' works have noted, was a Protestant minister who in the introduction to his edition declared Clamanges, d'Ailly, Gerson, and others to be proto-Reformers in line with Martin Luther's criticisms of the Roman Catholic Church a century later. For many codicological reasons, Lydius' collection is subject to much correction and was notably improved upon by two unpublished critical editions that surveyed, compared, and updated Clamanges' works through detailed analyses of manuscript sources. These are an epistolary edited by Dario Cecchetti in 1960 and a collection of treatises edited in

10. Dario Cecchetti, "L'elogio delle arti liberali nel primo umanesimo francese," *Studi Francesi* 28 (1966): 1–14; "Sulla fortuna del Petrarca in Francia: un testo dimenticato di Nicolas de Clamanges," *Studi Francesi* 31 (1967): 201–22; "'Florere-deflorescere.' In margine ad alcuni temi del primo umanesimo francese," in *Mélanges à la mémoire de Franco Simone. France et Italie dans la culture européene*, vol. 1, *Moyen Âge et Renaissance,* ed. H. Gaston Hall et al. (Geneva: Éditions Slatkine, 1980), 143–55; *Petrarca, Pietramala e Clamanges: storia di una "querelle" inventata* (Paris: Éditions CEMI, 1982); *L'evoluzione del latino umanistico in Francia* (Paris: Éditions CEMI, 1986); and "'Sic me Cicero laudare docuerat.' La retorica nel primo umanesimo francese," in *Préludes à la renaissance. Aspects de la vie intellectuelle en France au XVe siècle,* ed. Carla Bozzolo and Ezio Ornato (Paris: Éditions du CNRS, 1992), 47–106.

11. François Bérier, "L'humaniste, le prêtre et l'enfant mort: le sermon *'De sanctis innocentibus'* de Nicolas de Clamanges," in *L'Enfant au Moyen Âge (littérature et civilisation)* (Aix-en-Provence: Publications du CUERMA, 1980), 123–40; "La figure du clerc dans le *'De studio theologico'* de Nicolas de Clamanges," *Travaux de linguistique et de littérature* 21 (1983): 81–103; "Remarques sur le *'De Lapsu et Reparatione Iustitiae'* de Nicolas de Clamanges (vers 1360–1437) et sa traduction en française par F. Juret (1553–1626)," *Travaux de littérature* 3 (1990): 25–39; and "Remarques sur l'évolution des idées politiques de Nicolas de Clamanges," in *Pratiques de la culture écrite en France au XVe siècle,* ed. Monique Ornato and Nicole Pons (Louvain-la-Neuve: Fédération Internationale des Instituts d'Études Médiévales, 1995), 109–25.

two volumes by François Bérier in 1974.[12] These editions have been used as the textual basis for this study of the reform thought of Nicolas de Clamanges, to which we now turn.

12. These typescript editions were obtained through the graces of Gilbert Ouy and Louis B. Pascoe. Ouy, who directed Bérier's project and advised Cecchetti on his, considers their editions the most authoritative currently available: Ouy to author, 24 March 1994. Since these typescripts are difficult to obtain and Lydius' edition is available in a few libraries, parallel references to the Lydius edition will also be cited. The same procedure will be followed with regard to certain works by Clamanges which appear in other printed editions that the reader might also find more readily available. I am indebted to Bérier and Cecchetti's critical apparatus for their numerous identifications of Clamanges' scriptural and patristic sources on which I have relied while amending and supplementing them.

Part I

CHAPTER I

Life, Writings, Troubled Times

EARLY LIFE: THE CONTEXT OF AVIGNON AND THE SCHISM

On the cusp of some of the most contentious years of the Church's life, Nicolas de Clamanges was born Nicolas Poillevillain in 1363 or 1364 in Clamanges, a small village in the diocese of Châlons in Champagne. About 1375, Clamanges entered the University of Paris and began the arts curriculum in the prestigious Collège de Navarre, which was closely affiliated with the French monarchy and produced many influential scholars who tried to resolve the Schism and reform the Church. Both Clamanges and Gerson probably studied as protégés of d'Ailly, who was named rector of the Collège in 1384, chancellor of the University of Paris in 1389, bishop of Cambrai in 1397, and cardinal in 1411. Gerson succeeded d'Ailly as chancellor at the University of Paris in 1395. Together, d'Ailly and Gerson were leaders at the general council of Constance (1414–18). Despite the fact that d'Ailly and Gerson became Church statesmen while Clamanges ultimately turned away from the highest echelons of ecclesiastical politics, this troika remained close friends and maintained correspondence throughout their careers as they strove, each in his own way, to unite and reform the Church. Clamanges also developed lifelong personal and professional friendships with others at the Collège de Navarre who would play important roles in political, ecclesiastical, and intellectual matters at the University of Paris, the Avignon curia, and the French royal court. These friends included Gérard Machet (ca. 1380–1448), confessor of Charles VII and bishop of Castres; Jean de Montreuil (1353/54–1418), a royal ambassador who served as secretary to several members of France's ruling Valois family; and Jean Muret (d.

1419/20), papal secretary to Avignon's Clement VII and later canon at Mans.[1]

Clamanges' life was inextricably intertwined with the Avignon papacy and the Schism. His career frequently intersected with attempts by others to unite and reform the Church; these goals comprise the bulk of attention in his letters.[2] By the time of Clamanges' enrollment at Paris about 1375, the papacy had been thriving at Avignon for well over half a century. The papacy had settled in Avignon in 1309, four years after an eleven-month conclave in Perugia ended under the influence of Charles II of Anjou, the king of Naples. Upon his election at the conclusion of that long conclave, Clement V (1305–14) traveled throughout France and settled in Avignon, which was controlled by Charles II. France was safer for the papacy at the time because of two major expeditions by the Holy Roman Emperors into Italy. The 1310–13 invasion by Henry VII (1308–13) and the 1327–30 invasion by Lewis IV (1314–47) intensified the long-standing political split within Italy between the pro-imperial Ghibellines

1. For the details of Clamanges' life that inform the present chapter, see principally Bernstein, NP, and Ornato, *Jean Muret*. Less reliable are Palémon Glorieux, "Notations biographiques sur Nicolas de Clamanges," in *Mélanges offerts à M.-D. Chenu*, ed. André Duval (Paris: J. Vrin, 1967), 291–310; Kathleen Chesney, "Nicolas de Clamanges: Some Supplementary Biographical Notes," *Medium aevum* 7 (1938): 98–104; and P. Féret, *La Faculté de théologie de Paris et ses docteurs les plus célèbres. Moyen Âge*, 4 vols. (Paris: Picard, 1897), 4:279–95. On the Collège de Navarre, see Ferét, *La Faculté de théologie de Paris*, 3:10–18 with the founding charter at 3:599–600 and, more comprehensively, Nathalie Gorochov, *Le Collège de Navarre de sa fondation (1305) au début du XVe siècle (1418)* (Paris: Champion, 1997), with a biographical note on Clamanges at 616–18.

2. Lydius attributed 137 letters to Clamanges. Coville identified and edited thirteen more in *Recherches*, 282–317. Cecchetti's epistolary contains 143 letters, four of which may be classified as poems. Cecchetti subsequently edited seven more letters and re-edited others in "Nicolas de Clamanges e Gérard Machet. Contributo allo studio dell'epistolario di Nicolas de Clamanges," *Atti dell'Academia delle scienze di Torino* 100 (1965–66): 133–91, with texts at 183–91, and *L'evoluzione del latino umanistico in Francia* (Paris: Éditions CEMI, 1986), 96–123, 137–39. Glorieux included nine letters that Clamanges sent to Gerson in his *Jean Gerson. Oeuvres complètes*, 10 vols. (Paris: Desclée et Cie, 1960–73), 2:10–14, 50–53, 77–78, 116–23, 128–33, 142–50.

Selected groups of Clamanges' letters have been studied, but these articles generally examined his participation in humanism or politics. See principally André Combes, "Sur les 'lettres de consolation' de Nicolas de Clamanges à Pierre d'Ailly," *Archives d'histoire doctrinale et littéraire du Moyen Âge* 13 (1940–42): 359–89, and Pierre Santoni, "Les lettres de Nicolas de Clamanges à Gérard Machet. Un humaniste devant la crise du royaume et de l'Église (1410–1417)," *Mélanges de l'École française de Rome. Moyen Âge temps modernes* 99 (1987): 793–823.

and the pro-papal Guelphs, which led to factional wars, particularly in the papal states. At the same time in Avignon, the growth of an elaborate administrative bureaucracy, the luxurious living of curial prelates, and the predominance of French cardinals entrenched the papacy in southern France.

As the curia became known for its worldliness, there was strong sentiment that the papacy should return to Rome, its traditional seat, a sentiment promoted by Bridget of Sweden and Catherine of Siena. Despite threats by the French cardinals to abandon him, Urban V left Avignon for Italy in 1367, stayed briefly in Rome, and returned in late September 1370 to Avignon where he died three months later. Catherine of Siena pressed her case by meeting with Gregory XI in Avignon in 1376 to attack the financial and moral abuses there, and to exhort him to return the papacy to Rome permanently. For his part, Gregory XI was a skilled diplomat who was able to negotiate a measure of peace between Italy and the Holy Roman Empire, thereby paving the way for the papacy's return to the secure city of Rome and the papal states. Like Urban V before him, Gregory XI resisted pressure from the French cardinals to stay in Avignon. He entered Rome in January 1377, dying just more than one year later. Of the twenty-three cardinals who made up the Sacred College at the time of the conclave to elect his successor, sixteen were present in Rome and participated in the deliberations: eleven Frenchmen, four Italians, and one Spaniard. The residents of Rome were protective of the recently returned papacy and anxious to enjoy the prestige and financial benefits of a Roman curia once again. They even precipitated minor riots during Gregory XI's funeral. At the conclave's outset, leaders of Rome's neighborhoods reminded the cardinals that the concerns of the city's residents should be taken into account since the pope was also their metropolitan bishop. Split between two French cardinals, the conclave settled on an outside compromise candidate. Bartolomeo Prignano, the archbishop of Bari, appealed to both Italian and Avignon concerns: he was a native Neapolitan with Angevin political connections who had served in the Avignon curia for fifteen years. When the impatient Romans outside the conclave rioted once more, the frightened cardinals hastily devised a ruse: they vested the eighty-year-old Italian Cardinal Tebaldeschi as pope and presented him to the people. The cardinals then fled for safety to the Castel Sant'Angelo while the deceived crowd exulted. On 18 April 1378, Easter Sunday, Prignano was crowned as Urban VI with the papal tiara.

Urban VI quickly alienated his electors. He was born from a lower social class than the French cardinals, who considered him a petty bureaucrat rather than a curial prelate of their standing. Urban VI knew his canon law well, was admired for his austere spirituality, and promised to usher in necessary reforms, but his difficult personality led him to pursue laudable goals in a belligerent manner. From April to June 1378, he attacked absenteeism, particularly among the French cardinals who resided in Rome, and denounced their lavish lifestyles. Urban VI called the cardinal of Amiens greedy and physically assaulted him; he also fought with the cardinal of Milan and called another cardinal a half-wit. Led by Robert de Geneva, the Gallican candidate who had lost to Prignano in the conclave, the French cardinals in Rome claimed that the pope was not giving them proper respect and was diminishing their authority. The rift reached its moment of crisis by 21 June 1378 when all of the French cardinals had fled to Anagni. Out of Urban VI's grasp, they declared their election of Prignano canonically invalid on 9 August 1378 because it had been made in fear of the Roman mobs. When Urban VI sent a delegation of Italian bishops to negotiate, the French cardinals refused to discuss their differences. On 15 September 1378, they gathered in Fondi to elect a new pope; they were joined by several Italian cardinals lured from their allegiance to Urban VI by promises they would be considered prime candidates in conclave. On 20 September 1378, this conclave elected Robert de Geneva as pope; he took the name Clement VII and on 31 October 1378 was crowned with the papal tiara, as Urban VI had been. Clement VII and his cardinals were immediately excommunicated by Urban VI, who named twenty-eight new cardinals in their places.

Both popes called on military protection and hoped to settle the split by force of arms or excommunication. When Urban VI summoned his Roman supporters and won a military victory at Marino in the spring of 1379, Clement VII moved to Naples under the protection of Joanna I. Clement VII found the people of that city supported Urban VI, a

Neapolitan by birth, and so he moved to Avignon in June 1379 with the help of Joanna, whom Urban VI promptly excommunicated. With the papacies now physically separated, European allegiances lined up behind them. Obedient to Avignon were Sicily, Castile, and Scotland, the last in part because England supported Rome. Along with France's natural affinity for returning the papacy to her own soil, her political animosity toward England positioned her in Avignon's obedience since the two countries were embroiled in the intermittent Hundred Years War. The Roman obedience comprised England, Scandinavia, northern Italy, Germany, Hungary, Aragon, and Portugal, although Portugal's support was inconsistent, along with that of Venice, Bologna, and Milan.

UNIVERSITY AND CROWN: PARISIAN REACTIONS TO THE SCHISM

Clamanges' direct experience of the Schism was shaped by the University of Paris' reaction to the 1378 elections. Many academics at Paris, including d'Ailly, Gerson, and Clamanges, felt themselves pulled by competing loyalties. While the University of Paris was *parens scientiarum,* as Gregory IX had addressed her in 1231, Gerson noted she was also *filia regis.* Although for Gerson this characterization did not strictly subordinate the University to the king but indicated the academics' advisory role to their key patron, the relationship still stirred up dangerous waters for men like Clamanges and his friends to navigate, especially during the Schism.[3] Just about the time Clamanges was completing his arts studies, the University community split on the question of papal allegiance. A majority, especially the canon lawyers, supported Avignon's Clement VII; a strong and vocal minority of theologians backed the Roman Urban VI. Led by the Germans, these theologians sought a conciliar solution to the Schism and in 1379 the University of Paris advised

3. Pascoe, *Jean Gerson,* 80–82. R. N. Swanson provides an essential guide in *Universities, Academics and the Great Schism* (Cambridge: Cambridge University Press, 1979). Ideas on reform and union frequently circulated among academics, gaining a wider audience when the *magistri* played key roles in resolving the Schism: Jürgen Miethke, "Kirchenreform auf der Konzilien des 15. Jahrhunderts. Motive-Methoden-Wirkungen," in *Studien zum 15. Jahrhundert,* ed. Johannes Helmrath and Heribert Müller, 2 vols. (Munich: Oldenbourg, 1994), 1:28–39.

Charles V that it supported a general council of the Church to resolve the Schism. The French monarchy, however, pressured the University to back Clement VII and in May 1381 the bishop of Paris declared anyone who did not support the Avignon pope a schismatic heretic. That same year the new king, Charles VI, still in his minority and influenced by Valois family members, banned discussion of the Schism among the Parisian scholars. This regulation lasted almost a dozen years, and although it was periodically breached in debates or formal presentations of opinions, the ban had a chilling effect. Then, in July 1381 Clement VII replaced the chancellor of Paris with his own man, Jean Blanchard; later that year, the University of Paris formally accepted Clement VII as the pope. Most of the German conciliarists consequently left Paris in 1382 for home: Henry of Langenstein helped to establish the theology faculty at the University of Vienna and Conrad of Gelnhausen became rector at Heidelberg.

Clamanges was progressing through his studies at Paris and emerging as a notable scholar during these struggles. A Master of Arts in 1380, he began teaching in the arts faculty the next year while taking up theology studies. Although he was a Bachelor of Theology sometime between 1387 and 1394, Clamanges never became a Master of Theology like d'Ailly and Gerson even after returning to Paris and resuming theological studies near the end of his life. Like all academics at Paris, Clamanges accumulated benefices as sources of income. These included chaplaincies at the University of Paris and the high altar of Notre-Dame along with a canonry at St. Pierre de Lille; he was also canon and dean at St. Cloud and sought a position in his home diocese of Châlons.

While Clamanges progressed at Paris, the French royal family made an important switch in strategy. Despite its prior support for Avignon, as the Schism wore on the Valois did not wish to be labeled as schismatic and saw the rupture within the Church was preventing peace with England. The French crown's role in the Schism was complicated by the civil war that began early in Charles VI's reign. When Charles VI suffered one of his frequent bouts of insanity from 1380 until 1388, the duke of Burgundy, Philip the Bold, controlled his royal nephew. But when Charles VI was sane from 1388 to 1392, his younger brother Louis—who became the duke of Orléans in 1392—exercised dominant influence. In 1392, when Charles VI again became so mentally incompetent that Philip was named regent, the Burgundians moved to withdraw support for Clement VII in an attempt to force his abdication.[4]

Clamanges became an official of the University of Paris just as many of its scholars were also hardening their position toward Avignon. By 1394, his reputation for linguistic skills made him university *rédacteur* assigned with drawing up the academic community's official correspondence.[5] Most prominent was a letter that discussed their written opinions gathered during the winter of 1394. Once collated and studied by the chancellor d'Ailly and others, the opinions revealed the scholars supported three courses of action: a general council *(via concilii),* negotiation *(via compromissi),* and abdication *(via cessionis).* These three options were entrusted to Clamanges with the charge of using his considerable literary skills to draft the opinions into a persuasive and diplomatic letter to Charles VI; the letter, dated 6 June 1394, effectively governed attempts to reunite the Church for the next twenty years. It was delivered on 30 July 1394 to the king, who accepted it without comment; several weeks later, he rejected the three *viae* and reimposed his ban on discussion of the Schism at the University of Paris. Clement VII received a copy of the letter on 17 July 1394; he died two months later without responding. The Aragonese Pedro de Luna of the Avignon obedience was elected to succeed him, taking the name Benedict XIII. As a candidate in conclave, de Luna had hinted he might resign for the sake of unifying the Church,

4. Howard Kaminsky, *Simon de Cramaud and the Great Schism* (New Brunswick, N.J.: Rutgers University Press, 1983), 25–65.

5. Nine letters that were probably drafted by Clamanges are in C. Du Boulay, ed., *Historia Universitatis Parisiensis,* 5 vols. (Paris, 1665–73), 4:687–96, 699–705, 711–16, 721–22. Four of these nine are also in H. Denifle and E. Châtelain, eds., *Chartularium Universitatis Parisiensis,* 4 vols. (Paris: 1889–97), 3:617–25, 629–36. One of these nine was discussed and re-edited by Combes, *Jean de Montreuil et le chancelier Gerson* (Paris: J. Vrin, 1942), 625–33. Two versions of a tenth letter are in d'Achery 1:795–98 and 6:143. Lydius offered one letter in L 1:187–90. See the treatment of the University of Paris letters in C xxx–xxxiv, where Cecchetti attributes nine to Clamanges; B 1:ix–xi, where Bérier also identifies nine; and Bernstein, NP, 6–7 and 56–57 where he lists ten. Clamanges' official letters for the University of Paris have not been attributed definitively to him. Even if they are, however, a vexing problem remains: determining the degree to which they represent Clamanges' own opinions in draft form or the thoughts of the Parisian academics who edited them.

but once elected he quickly became the most obstinate of popes. In response to his refusal to abdicate, a council of Paris voted 87–22 in favor of Benedict XIII's resignation in February 1395, but this move immediately became a dead letter when the new Avignon pope refused to step down.

Clamanges' rising career did not falter despite the University's opposition to the Avignon papacy and his role in the 6 June 1394 letter. Benedict XIII, perhaps looking to curry favor among Parisian leaders who might otherwise prove formidable foes, named Clamanges his secretary on 16 November 1397; he also added a canonry at Langres to Clamanges' benefices.[6] Clamanges embraced the considerable advances in humanistic scholarship he found in the Avignon curia, but at the same time was greatly disturbed by the greed he witnessed there. In addition, he was quickly caught between allegiance to his Parisian friends and the opportunities offered by the papal curia. Just as he was entering the inner circles of Avignon, the University of Paris and the Valois family were strengthening their positions against Benedict XIII by moving closer to a withdrawal of obedience: refusal to recognize his spiritual authority and to pay papal revenues. A vote to withdraw obedience taken at a council of Paris in the summer of 1396 had failed, but the voice of moderation against withdrawal led by d'Ailly quickly dissipated. The withdrawal of obedience was finally approved and implemented at the council of Paris in July 1398.[7]

6. As with the University of Paris' official correspondence, Clamanges' letters for Benedict XIII have not been critically edited or even attributed to him beyond doubt. Bernstein lists seven that may have come from his hand: NP, 58. Various versions are in d'Achery 1:787–90, 794–95, 800, 805–806; and 6:120, 123, 126, 157, 164, 178, 188. Lydius included four letters for Benedict XIII in L 1:179–86.

7. On the councils of Paris, see Hélène Millet, "Du conseil au concile (1395–1408). Recherche sur le nature des assemblées du clergé en France pendant le Grand Schisme d'Occident," *Journal des savants* (1985): 137–59; and Millet and Emmanuel Poulle, *Le vote de la soustraction d'obédience en 1398, I: Introduction. Édition et facsimilés des bulletins du vote* (Paris: CNRS, 1988). For royal and university strategies, see Kaminsky, *Simon de Cramaud*, 178–243, and Swanson, *Universities, Academics and the Great Schism*, 90–134. D'Ailly's efforts against the withdrawal in 1395 and 1396 are discussed in Christopher M. Bellitto, "The Early Development of Pierre d'Ailly's Conciliarism," *Catholic Historical Review* 83 (1997): 223–30.

FIRST ACTIVE EXILE: FIGHTING THE
SUBTRACTION OF OBEDIENCE

The years 1398–1403 when the withdrawal of obedience was in effect were difficult for those opposed to the measure, among them Clamanges, d'Ailly, and Gerson, who spent this period in prudent retreats from Paris. Clamanges passed the time at Langres, having left Avignon just before the July 1398 vote. In May 1398, he had fallen gravely ill and almost died of plague at Avignon; on 22 June 1398 Benedict XIII had sent Clamanges to his Langres canonry. At d'Ailly's suggestion, Clamanges wrote a treatise on Church reform: *De ruina et reparacione Ecclesie (On the Ruin and Renewal of the Church)*, ca. 1400–1401.[8] In *De ruina* and his early letters, Clamanges expressed ideas and images which resounded throughout his later writings. At length, he decried the state of the Church in head and members, laid down principles for reform, and warned of the Church's imminent destruction if the reforms he urged were not accomplished.

Clamanges' first active exile deserves particular attention because it reveals how Benedict XIII fit Clamanges into the political negotiations to restore obedience, a topic which Clamanges addressed often from Langres. Ostensibly, Benedict XIII had sent Clamanges to Langres to recuperate after an almost fatal bout of plague. Clamanges at that time also declared he was grateful to have escaped the curial corruption he witnessed in Avignon.[9] In addition, Clamanges surely welcomed the retreat because it removed him from the center of the estranged relationship between the Avignon papacy on the one hand, and the University of Paris, the Valois family, and the French clergy on the other. But there is

8. Coville critically edited *De ruina* in *Le Traité*, 111–56. *De ruina* is *De corrupto Ecclesiae statu* in L 1:4–28. Constantin Fasolt translated excerpts from Coville's edition for *Medieval Europe*, ed. Julius Kirshner and Karl F. Morrison (Chicago: University of Chicago Press, 1986), 434–46. A. Müntz concluded Clamanges was not the author of *De ruina* in *Nicolas de Clémanges, sa vie et ses écrits* (Strasbourg, 1846). His contention was rebutted by G. Schuberth's dissertation, *Nicolaus von Clemanges, der Verfasser der Schrift De Corrupto ecclesiae statu* (Grossenhaim, 1888); see also Coville, *Le Traité*, 13–15. Müntz was systematically refuted by Peter Hemmerle, "Nikolaus Poillevillain, gennant Nikolaus von Clemanges und die Schrift, 'De corrupto ecclesiae statu,'" *Historisches Jahrbuch* 27 (1906): 803–12; see also Bernstein, NP, 33 n. 75.

9. C 95.62–66 (L 2:58).

some question about why Clamanges abandoned the curia during the withdrawal of obedience since he vehemently opposed it. While it seems plausible that the withdrawal was Clamanges' excuse to leave a curia whose immorality he found offensive and whose excesses he chronicled in detail, Clamanges rejoined the Avignon curia when obedience was restored in 1403. Ezio Ornato believes Clamanges abandoned Avignon in 1398 with some hesitation even though he was concerned about curial practices. But he prudently waited out the political storm surrounding the withdrawal by using poor health as a pretext: in this way, Clamanges was able to profess judicious but not contradictory loyalty to his pope, his king, and the University of Paris under the rationale of convalescence. Benedict XIII may have seen the withdrawal as inevitable in November 1397 and deliberately provided Clamanges with a safe retreat that would allow him to survive financially. More importantly, Clamanges would have been in Benedict XIII's debt and in a favorable position to promote the restoration of obedience to the Avignon papacy, which he did not fail to do.[10]

Clamanges' principal objection to the withdrawal pertained to the loss of order and obedience for the Church. In a letter to Benedict XIII obviously intended to give the Avignon pope arguments with which to defend himself in the summer of 1398, Clamanges employed Paul's well-known image of the Church as one body with its head united integrally to its many members (1 Cor 12:12–27). Obedience gave cohesion, order, discipline, and virtue to the Church as a body. Without obedience, vice and evil would run free; danger and scandal would infect the body. If the Church's authority at her head were to be removed, the members would no longer obey the head; lower prelates could not command obedience if the pope was not being obeyed by his own men. When the head lost its vitality, the members would wither and the entire Church would be more easily exposed to her enemies. Since obedience flowed from the head of the hierarchy into its lower grades, Clamanges asked rhetorically, would not withdrawing obedience from the top of the ecclesiastical order lead to withdrawal of obedience from the entire body of the Church?[11]

10. Ornato, *Jean Muret,* 53–66.
11. C 87.177–82, 88.205–18, 88.224–89.231 (L 2:53, 54).

Clamanges also pronounced himself confounded by certain prelates and doctors (presumably at Paris) who agreed with the Valois strategy of forcing Benedict XIII's abdication through the withdrawal. They supported the move but failed to see it would only continue the Schism and restrict ecclesiastical liberty; they were unconcerned with the effects that would imperil not only the Church but their own comfortable positions. Blinded by greed, they were convinced their incomes and prestige would increase because they would not be under papal authority. Clamanges concluded with dismay and frustration that greedy men concerned not for the safety of the Church but only with filling their own pockets would unwittingly produce desolation and ruin for the Church and themselves.

Clamanges also opposed the withdrawal on pastoral and political grounds. If the Church became a slave to secular authority, as he warned would occur, the Church's sheep would disperse. Once the shepherd had been struck, the sheep would be sent to the jaws of surrounding wolves; no one could save the sheep from their bite. In his letter to Benedict XIII, Clamanges informed the cardinals that as a result of the loss of ecclesiastical liberty no one would seek their influence by offering benefices. The cardinals would be ridiculed and condemned, only prospering if they became "yes men" *(assentatores)* to secular princes. Who of episcopal or inferior rank, he asked, would seek such oppression?[12]

After the subtraction had been put into effect, Clamanges continued to argue against the move in letters from Langres. He told Gerson that his predictions about the subtraction had come true and promised that clerics siding with earthly authority would be punished as if struck by a bolt of heavenly lightning. He fulminated against men who failed to understand the perils to ecclesiastical dignity: they were still ignorant of the dangers they brought on themselves and the Church through secular entanglements and dominance. Although secular rulers were ministers of God entrusted with defending the faith, they violated the Church by working against her order, liberty, and sanctity. The king, the servant of God who should protect the Church, failed to see that through the withdrawal he opposed God, incurring divine wrath and penalty. Just as he

12. C 85.108–86.145 (L 2:52–53), following Zec 13:7, Mt 26:31, Mk 14:27; C 86.150–87.173 (L 2:53); C 87.183–88 (L 2:54); C 89.252–59 (L 2:55).

wished his own inferiors to be obedient to him, the king should obey God. How much more could the king harm the Church than by intruding into her affairs, by going against the principle of free canonical election, and by appointing unworthy men who sought positions only because of ambition?[13]

Clamanges took these complaints straight to the king in a long letter in 1402. Because all were blind to the current troubles, from active exile Clamanges set out to prove to Charles VI that the withdrawal had been a terrible mistake, that it was a persistent failure, and that the king should work toward restoring obedience. As he had done with Gerson, Clamanges told the king the withdrawal produced precisely those situations which Clamanges feared from the beginning and against which he had warned specifically in his 1398 letter to Benedict XIII. Disorder, the Schism, and secular encroachments on ecclesiastical dignity and liberty persisted, but Benedict XIII still remained on the papal throne in Avignon in 1402. While it lasted, the withdrawal of obedience served only as another impediment to union.[14] In four years the withdrawal accomplished nothing positive. Clamanges cited one of Augustine's sermons to drive home an ominous message concerning the fact that sin and scandal persisted because of the withdrawal. While it may be human to err, Augustine had noted in discussing the Donatists, it was diabolical to remain in error through animosity. This citation was a respectful warning to the king: though he may be excused for allowing the withdrawal, Charles VI must not permit the troubles it produced to continue.[15] Throughout Church and kingdom, the move increased turmoil, danger, and lack of faith. Nothing would persist except confusion, scandal, and

13. C 181.18–24, 32–50 (L 2:108); C 182.62–72 (L 2:108), following Rom 13:4; C 182.82–183.94 (L 2:109).

14. C 104.127–38 (L 2:63).

15. C 101.19–33 (L 2:62, correcting an error in the pagination of Lydius' edition), quoting Augustine, *Sermo* 164.14 in PL 38.901–2: *"Humanum fuit errare, diabolicum est per animositatem in errore manere."* Augustine then addressed the Donatists' deceit, self-deceit, and the necessity for the correction of their own and others' errors. See PL 38.902: *"Melius quidem erat si nunquam erraremus: sed vel quod secundum est faciamus, ut errorem aliquando emendemus. Decepimus, quia decepti eramus: falsa praedicavimus, qui praedicantibus falsa credidimus. . . . Simul erravimus, simul ab errore recedamus. Duces vobis fuimus ad foveam, et secuti estis cum duceremus ad foveam* (Lk 6:39); *et nunc sequimini cum ducimus ad Ecclesiam."* Clamanges did not cite these sentences but discussed similar issues in the rest of this letter to Charles VI.

dict XIII: Charles VI would declare France neutral in the Schism if union was not achieved by the Feast of the Ascension, 24 May 1408. In response, on 18 April 1408 Benedict XIII issued a bull excommunicating Charles VI. One month later, the bull was torn to shreds with the approval and in the presence of the king and representatives of the University of Paris. After thirty years of tentative support and disagreement, on 25 May 1408—just one day after the Ascension Day deadline—the French royal family definitively broke off its relationship with the Avignon papacy and declared France neutral in the Schism.[22]

Parisian scholars and royal supporters immediately accused Clamanges of writing the papal bull of excommunication. He tried to prove his innocence in five 1408 letters sent to various parties in Paris in which he zealously defended himself. His efforts to resolve the Schism and reform the Church did not deserve unjust attacks, Clamanges declared, and accusations against him should cease. In fact, he countered, his actions should instead be praised. Clamanges even self-righteously took comfort in applying to himself Jesus' statement that a prophet is not without honor except in his own country. He said he specifically objected when some Parisians dared to match his literary elegance to that of the bull. His pen proved the writing in the bull was alien to his own characteristic style; this fact alone should free him from suspicion.[23] Whether the accusation against Clamanges was justified remains an open question, but the bull clearly widened the break between the members of the University of Paris community and Clamanges which, according to Ezio Ornato, had been building since late 1397. Clamanges' exit from Paris to join the Avignon curia at that time may have later been interpreted by some university scholars as the first sign of treason that

22. Benedict XIII's bull was actually dated 19 May 1407 because a partial withdrawal of obedience had been planned by a royal ordinance dated 18 February 1407. Although this ordinance was never promulgated, Benedict knew of its existence and prepared the bull in May 1407 as a counter attack: he strategically held it in reserve until the king's January 1408 threat.

23. The five letters are in C 209–32 (L 2:127–42); see especially 217.106–16 (L 2:133), following Mt 13:57, Jn 4:44; C 219.48–69 (L 2:134); C 223.84–224.140 (L 2:136–37). Cecchetti cites Clamanges' defense of himself on the point of style: "'*Sic me Cicero laudare docuerat.*' La retorica nel primo umanesimo francese," in *Préludes à la Renaissance. Aspects de la vie intellectuelle en France au XVe siècle,* ed. Carla Bozzolo and Ezio Ornato (Paris: CNRS, 1992), 54 n. 32.

was sealed by the bull. Ornato reviewed the charges that Clamanges wrote or participated in the writing of the bull along with Clamanges' defenses. By a close examination of the matter and its context, he concluded that despite Clamanges' strenuous protestations of innocence it is difficult to doubt the core charge: he had exhibited a measure of animosity toward the Valois.[24]

Whatever his role in the bull, Clamanges' frustration with Benedict XIII's obstinacy toward resolving the Schism had grown strong by 1408. In December 1407 or early 1408, he abandoned Benedict XIII's service while traveling with him in Italy. During 1408, Clamanges shuttled between Paris and Avignon trying to clear his name and find a way out of difficult circumstances. Unwelcome in Paris and disgusted with Avignon, Clamanges spent some time at the Carthusian monastery at Valprofond near Béon before moving more permanently to the Augustinian priory of Ste-Mary Magdelene in Fontaine-au-Bois near Provins. Apparently soured by his costly experiences in academic, civil, and ecclesiastical politics, Clamanges spent the next ten years (1408–1418) in a prolific second exile, mostly at Fontaine-au-Bois, writing on reform. Because of particularly intense political intrigue relating to the French civil war, Clamanges passed several months in Langres in 1412 and 1413. He refused overtures to return to Benedict XIII's service in 1413 and to enter Charles VI's chancery in 1414.[25]

In his second and longer active exile, Clamanges expounded on many of the themes of personal and pastoral reform he had begun to develop during his first active exile. His large volume of letters and treatises demonstrates he was quite involved in the events of his day even though he was geographically separated from the centers of power. Building on his own difficult experiences, Clamanges emphasized a *reformatio personalis* upon which the lasting reform of the entire Church depended. This accent is especially clear in a 1410 treatise praising the solitary life,

24. Ornato, *Jean Muret*, 178–81, 188. Bernstein is also unconvinced by Clamanges' protestations of innocence: NP, 15–16, especially n. 91.

25. Clamanges seems to have maintained his personal regard for his patron Benedict XIII but, with his Parisian colleagues, became frustrated with the Avignon pope's reluctance to compromise or abdicate in order to resolve the Schism: Ornato, *Jean Muret*, 133–34.

De fructu heremi (On the Fruits of the Eremitical Life)[26] and another on the cultivation of virtues, *De prosperitate aduersitatis (On the Prosperity of Adversity)*[27] ca. 1407–12. These two treatises were clearly influenced by the isolation and opposition Clamanges felt as he tried to steer a middle course among the Avignon papacy, the Parisian academic community, and the French royal family. Also dating from Clamanges' exiles are the sermons *De sanctis innocentibus (On the Holy Innocents)*[28] and *De filio prodigo (On the Prodigal Son)*,[29] both ca. 1402–14, and a treatise entitled *De nouis festiuitatibus non instituendis (On Not Instituting New Feasts)*[30] from 1413. Clamanges especially considered the training and conduct of clergy charged with pastoral care during his second active exile. He offered his recommendations on reforming the scandals of priestly hypocrisy and faithlessness in a 1412 treatise sent to Gerson, *Contra prelatos symoniacos (Against Simoniacal Prelates)*.[31] Clamanges provided both a description of the problems the Church faced and a prescription particularly focused on the pastoral needs of Christians. Because the theoretical excesses of scholasticism led scholars and clerics to lose sight of what Clamanges saw as their main role as faith-filled teachers, he launched an attack on this trend in *De studio theologico (On Theological Study)* about 1412.[32] There, he presented his views on the personal preparation and pastoral education of parish priests, which emphasized training for the *cura animarum*.

Some time during the period of Clamanges' two active exiles and his public career he wrote several more works. One was a poem addressing the Church's problems, which reflected his reform writings and summarized his *De ruina* from ca. 1400–1401: *Deploratio calamitatis ecclesiastice*

26. B 2:26–46 (L 1:121–32).

27. B 2:47–68 (L 1:132–43, titled *De fructu rerum adversarum*).

28. B 2:159–76, otherwise unedited; Bérier, "L'humaniste, le prêtre et l'enfant mort: le sermon *'De sanctis innocentibus'* de Nicolas de Clamanges," in *L'Enfant au Moyen Âge (littérature et civilisation)* (Aix-en-Provence: Publications du CUERMA, 1980), 123–40.

29. B 2:1–25 (L 1:109–21).

30. B 2:69–103 (L 1:143–60, titled *De nouis celebritatibus non instituendis*); Glorieux, "Moeurs de la Chrétienté au temps de Jeanne d'Arc: le *'Traité contre l'institution de fêtes nouvelles'* de Nicolas de Clamanges," *Mélanges de sciences religieuses* 23 (1966): 15–29.

31. B 2:136–48 (L 1:160–66, titled *De praesulibus simoniacis*).

32. B 2:104–35 (d'Achery 1:473–80).

(Lamentation on the Calamity Afflicting the Church).[33] Clamanges wrote a poetic *Descriptio et laus urbis Ianue (Description and Praise of the City of Genoa),* probably in 1405 while accompanying Benedict XIII in Italy.[34] He composed ten prayers during the second active exile: using the Cistercian Bernard of Clairvaux (1090–1153) as a spiritual guide, Clamanges linked the canonical hours of prayer with the gifts of the Holy Spirit.[35] Clamanges also wrote the *Histoire de Floridan et d'Elvide,* a humanistic love story dated very roughly 1397–1408 that inspired later versions.[36] He began to collect his letters and to revise his treatises near the end of this second exile, ca. 1414–18.[37]

CONCILIAR PERIOD AND FINAL YEARS

During the time of Clamanges' second active exile of 1408–18, attempts to resolve the Schism continued by means of general councils. In 1409, cardinals from the Avignon and Roman obediences met at Pisa and declared their two popes deposed. They then unanimously elected the Greek Franciscan Pietro Philarghi (Peter of Candia) as Alexander V. Instead of resolving the Schism, however, Europe was simply split further into three obediences. Because of the failure of Pisa, another general council was held at Constance (1414–18). None of the popes had wanted to call a general council for fear of deposition, but the Holy Roman Emperor-elect Sigismund, eager for union and the title of universal pro-

---

33. C 645–68 (L 1:32–36) and Coville, *Recherches,* 261–64. Cecchetti disagrees with Coville's dating of the poem to 1408: he concurs it was written during the Schism, but asserts a precise date cannot be determined: C lxxxiv.

34. To Clamanges are also attributed the poems *Descriptio vite rustice* (*Description of the Rustic Life*) and *Descriptio vite tirannice* (*Description of the Tyrannical Life*) from 1394. These two poems are not original to Clamanges but are Latin translations of two French texts: Philippe de Vitry's *Dit de Franc-Gontier* and d'Ailly's *Contredit de Franc-Gontier.* For analysis and critical editions, see Cecchetti, "'*Descriptio loci*' e '*Laudatio urbis.*' Persistenza e rinnovamento di strutture retoriche nell'opera di Nicolas de Clamanges," *Annali dell'Istituto Universitario Orientale* 35 (1993): 381–431.

35. Jean Leclercq, "Les prières inédites de Nicolas de Clamanges," *Revue d'ascétique et de mystique* 23 (1947): 171–83; Bérier, "Note sur la datation, la tradition manuscrite et le contenu des dix oraisons de l'humaniste Nicolas de Clamanges," in *La Prière au Moyen Âge (littérature et civilisation)* (Paris: Champion, 1981), 7–25.

36. B 2:149–58. On the content and influence of this love story, see Coville, *Recherches,* 208–44.

37. C xxxix and B 1:xlviii–xlix.

tector of the Church, promised Alexander's successor John XXIII protection. John XXIII called the council of Constance, confident he could control its deliberations with Sigismund's backing. The Roman pope Gregory XII sent two delegates in his name. Benedict XIII played no part in the council and did not dispatch any representatives to Constance.

The delegates at Constance laid down three tasks: the *causae unionis, fidei, et reformationis*. The *causa fidei* centered on the posthumous declaration of John Wycliffe as a heretic in May 1415 and the trial, condemnation, and execution of Jan Hus for heresy in June and July 1415. The *causa reformationis* was largely subordinated to the resolution of the Schism, although several committees of delegates at Constance drafted legislation to abolish simony and its attendant problems of absenteeism and pluralism; to secure a more rigorous *examinatio* of candidates for priesthood and ecclesiastical offices; and to ensure a higher degree of moral standards and behavior among the clergy. Most reform proposals, however, remained unlegislated because of the more immediate need to resolve the Schism, and the attempts by the delegates to justify their conciliar authority and actions.

The primary item of business at Constance was the *causa unionis*. The hope was the three popes would peacefully resign. Benedict XIII refused but Gregory XII indicated through his delegates he would be willing to step down. John XXIII agreed to resign as well, most likely because he expected to be reelected. When this possibility came into doubt, John XXIII fled Constance on 20 March 1415, calculating the council's validity would be questioned by his absence. Three days later, Gerson in his sermon on John 12:35, *Ambulate dum lucem habetis,* provided the delegates with the theological grounds for continuing. The general council, he argued, was led by the Holy Spirit and not one particular pope. Representing the Church, the council validated itself by the grace of the Holy Spirit; even the pope must follow its actions. These theological grounds were set more legalistically on 6 April 1415 in the conciliar decree *Haec sancta synodus,* which declared a general council represents the Church and receives its legitimate authority from the Holy Spirit and Christ. The general council, then, was superior to the pope, who could be punished for challenging or failing to heed the general council's pronouncements, including any made in matters of faith.

The council delegates now moved quickly to resolve the Schism. They deposed John XXIII on 29 May 1415 and threatened Gregory XII with the same. The Roman pope's delegates negotiated a compromise: they formally reconvoked the council in his name, preserving a measure of recognition of his claim to legitimacy, and then Gregory XII resigned on 4 July 1415. Benedict XIII, however, remained true to his character and steadfastly resisted even after Sigismund visited him in Spain. Most of his supporters deserted him, but he never recognized the general council at Constance or the pope it elected as legitimate. He was deposed two years later on 26 July 1417, though he maintained his claim to be the true pope until his death in 1423. After Benedict XIII's deposition, the delegates approved the decree *Frequens,* which was designed to keep conciliar authority alive by making regular the meetings of general councils. A three day conclave consisting of cardinals from all three previous obediences and council delegates then elected Cardinal Odo Colonna, obedient to the Pisan papacy, as Martin V in November 1417. The Church, after nearly forty years, finally claimed a single and unifying pope.

These great conciliar events did not pass Clamanges by. He was not uninvolved with the deliberations at Constance, writing five letters to the delegates. Three letters written in July 1415 were gathered together by Lydius as the *Disputatio super materia concilii generalis (A Disputation on the Matter of the General Council).* In order to understand Clamanges' opinions on the council of Constance fully, to those three letters should be added an earlier letter dating from late 1414 or January 1415 and another from the second half of 1416. These letters were not intricate legalistic or theoretical texts on conciliar authority: Clamanges principally reminded the delegates to keep reform and the pastoral needs of Christians foremost in their minds as they deliberated with the Holy Spirit's aid.[38]

Clamanges' precise whereabouts from the last months of the general council of Constance until his appearance in Paris in 1423 are not cer-

38. C 519–50 (L 1:60–79); C 486–94 (L 2:290–94); C 550–58 (L 2:310–14).

tain. We know he was in Constance sometime after the November 1417 election of Martin V because the new pope named him papal secretary. Although Clamanges functioned as papal secretary for some time, it is not clear he joined Martin V during the pope's two-year journey in northern Italy following his departure from Constance in May 1418.[39] Clamanges soon wished to return to Paris more than he wanted to be entangled in the papal curia again, but his life intersected with the events of the French civil war once more. The house of Burgundy's favor would have been necessary to guarantee Clamanges' safe return to the Collège de Navarre because of recent events. On 28–29 May 1418, matters turned violent when the Burgundians entered Paris, chased the dauphin from the city, and launched an assault against his supporters. Their targets included the Collège de Navarre: they pillaged its library and took many prisoners whom they later massacred. In response, supporters of the dauphin assassinated John the Fearless in 1419. As these events transpired, Clamanges composed a treatise on the civil war, *De lapsu et reparacione iustitiae (On the Decline and Renewal of Justice)*. Completed in 1420, the treatise demonstrated his desire for a peaceful resolution to the civil war for the sake of the Church and French society. He sent the work to Philip the Good, John the Fearless' son and successor as duke of Burgundy, evidently attempting to cultivate Philip's favor in light of the Anglo-Burgundian alliance sealed by the Treaty of Troyes in 1420.[40] In a

39. Bernstein has wondered why Clamanges, content in exile and chastened by his previous political experiences, would have rejoined the papal curia: NP, 22–25. Bérier provides evidence that Clamanges functioned as papal secretary to Martin V in 1418. In that year Clamanges sent a collection of his works to Alfonso V of Aragon with a letter that contained the incipit: *"Epistola N. de Clamengiis Pape secretarii . . ."*: B 1:lii and 2:appendix I.

40. Bernstein, NP, 23, and Bernstein to author, 29 October 1994. The printed text is in L 1:41–59 (correcting an error in the pagination of Lydius' edition). See Bérier, "Remarques sur le *'De lapsu et reparatione iustitiae'* de Nicolas de Clamanges (vers 1360–1437) et sa traduction en française par F. Juret (1555–1626)," *Travaux de littérature* 3 (1990): 25–39, and "Remarques sur l'évolution des idées politiques de Nicolas de Clamanges," in *Pratiques de la culture écrite en France au XVe siècle*, ed. Monique Ornato and Nicole Pons (Louvain-la-Neuve: Fédération Internationale des Instituts d'Études Médiévales, 1995), 109–25. On the difficult political context of Clamanges' return to the Collège de Navarre, see Jacques Verger, "The University of Paris at the End of the Hundred Years' War," in *Universities in Politics: Case Studies from the Late Middle Ages and Early Modern Period*, ed. John W. Baldwin and Richard A. Goldthwaite (Baltimore: Johns Hopkins University Press, 1972), 47–78, and Gorochov, *Le Collège de Navarre*, 561–72.

letter to Henry V in late 1417 or January 1418, Clamanges may also have been trying to protect his Bayeux benefice since it was in English-held territory at that time.[41]

About 1423 Clamanges returned to Paris, where he taught the arts once again, worked on editions of his writings, and resumed theological studies that produced a long but unfinished commentary on the Book of Isaiah: *Expositio super quadraginta septem capitula Isaie.*[42] From 1425 until 1434, Clamanges served the Collège de Navarre as provisor. His calls for reform continued with renewed urgency, as may be attested by two very brief treatises dating from about 1430: *De Antichristo et ortu eius, vita, moribus et operibus (On the Antichrist and His Birth, Life, Ways and Deeds)*[43] and *Exhortatio ad resistendum contra Machometicos (Exhortation to Resist Muslims).*[44] Clamanges died in 1437, only two years after the long civil war in France ended with the Treaty of Arras between Charles VII (1422–61) and the Burgundians. He was buried in front of the main altar in the chapel of the Collège de Navarre, his home at the University of Paris.

41. C 641.249–56 (L 2:351); Bérier, "Remarques sur l'évolution des idées politiques," 116.

42. There is only one manuscript (Paris, Arsenal MS 137) and no critical edition, although Bérier continues to work on this project. Coville introduces the unfinished and repetitive *Expositio* in *Le Traité,* 91–106. See Bérier, "Exégèse et ironie: À propos de l'*'Expositio super quadraginta septem capitula Ysaye'* de Nicolas de Clamanges (ca. 1425)," *Recherches et travaux. Université de Grenoble Bulletin* 41 (1991): 17–35; "Remarques sur l'*'Expositio super quadraginta septem capitula Isaie'* de Nicolas de Clamanges: Genèse de l'oeuvre, datation, méthode et contenu," in *L'Hostellerie de pensée,* ed. Michel Zink and Danielle Bohler (Paris: Presses de l'Université de Paris-Sorbonne, 1995), 41–49, where he contends this treatise may have been planned or even begun in late 1413; and "Remarques sur l'évolution des idées politiques," 120–23.

43. B 2:177–81 and C 657–61 (L 2:357–59).

44. B 2:182–86 and C 661–65.

CHAPTER 2

The Reformer at Work

🌿

Clamanges' life and writings were inseparably linked with a Church in great need of comprehensive reform, so we must first treat the themes, images, and fears that undergird his reform program. Despite the extreme difficulties facing the Church he described, Clamanges trusted Christians could address the need to reform her. His faith in humanity's ability to act was justified by principles of patristic and medieval humanism that greatly influenced how Clamanges envisioned the interplay between divine grace and human action in reforming the late medieval Church. Finally, we must consider how Clamanges saw himself as best meeting the tasks of reform.

IMAGES OF A TROUBLED CHURCH

Clamanges frequently expressed his reform images in dark, gloomy, and pessimistic rhetoric. He asserted the Church's problems were her own fault: she tainted herself through the Schism, greed, and lack of pastoral care. Worldly ministers in head and members were ignorant of the damage they had done to the Church. In his earliest reform treatise, *De ruina et reparacione Ecclesie,* he noted with trepidation that every level and grade within the Church was broken up, confounded, dissolved, and languished. As in Noah's day, there was little to admire: lies and crimes were common, sincerity and innocence were rare. The arrogance and pride of churchmen coupled with the effects of the Schism slowly brought the Church to ruin. Their vices also invited divine wrath: ecclesiastics would receive torments in proportion to how much they delighted in their worldliness.[1] Clamanges painted a similarly bleak picture of

1. Coville, *Le Traité,* 145, following Gn 6:11–13; 147, 148, 150. Clamanges repeated this warning from Marseilles several years later after he had rejoined Benedict XIII's curia: C 200.162–201.180 (L 2:119–20), following Sir 15:14, Ps 7:16, Prov 1:27, 31.

the Church for Charles VI in 1402 when he described the weakening of faith, hope, charity, justice, piety, and truth. Throughout the Church, order was upset, freedoms were impaired, and reason was spurned while ambitions and desires reigned over modesty. The situations were so bad, he complained to d'Ailly about the same time, it was difficult to deplore or exaggerate them enough. With so many troubles inside the Church, Clamanges asked rhetorically a decade later in *Contra prelatos symoniacos,* was it any wonder that the Church was still despised, hated, afflicted, and oppressed?[2]

The taproot of these troubles within the Church was greed, especially with respect to simony. Writing ca. 1408–11 from his second active exile, Clamanges bemoaned the fact that simony was extolled as the highest pastoral skill, but was in reality the deadliest plague in the Church. From this pestilence many additional troubles flowed among the clergy, including knowledge of civil matters to the exclusion of Christ's law, poor moral conduct, and worldly ambition. In an earlier letter to Gerson written after his first experience of curial life at Avignon, Clamanges noted that even virtuous and honest servants of the Church were attacked because of their simoniacal colleagues.[3] He fully manifested his concern with simony, immorality, and the lack of pastoral care in *Contra prelatos symoniacos,* where he stressed that the many vices introduced by the criminal traffic in spiritual offices greatly confused and disgraced the Church. He addressed simoniacal prelates directly with a more serious charge: by not following the proper path and by disregarding divine law, they provided perverse examples and dragged others into the pit of Gehenna with them. Because of them, the Church was beset by thieves like the man on his way from Jerusalem to Jericho.[4]

Greed and vice troubled the Church on the local level where parish priests emulated the poor examples set by greedy, negligent prelates. Though *De ruina* was written in the aftermath of Clamanges' first period of curial service and is characterized mostly by a concern with the head of the Church, he also singled out for criticism *in membris* monks,

2. C 117.595–99 (L 2:71); C 175.22–25 (L 2:104); B 2:147.315–17 (L 1:165).
3. C 364.177–365.186 (L 2:223); C 184.123–26 (L 2:109).
4. B 2:138.63–66 (L 1:161); B 2:144.235–38 (L 1:164); B 2:147.327–32 (L 1:165), following Lk 10:30–37.

nuns, friars, and canons of cathedral chapters. He charged monks with exhibiting worldliness that was far from the spiritual perfection their rules and vows would have cultivated had they been followed. Few were faithful to the monastic life at all; their houses literally fell into disrepair because they spent money elsewhere. Clamanges criticized nuns in shocking terms by describing them as being more like prostitutes. Because convents were closer to brothels, veiling a young girl was akin to exposing her to public scandal.

Some of his most stinging complaints attacked mendicant friars who claimed to be the only true ministers in the Church, but who in fact preferred worldly glory to divine service. Their virtue vanished as soon as they extolled themselves. Clamanges accused them of being like the Pharisees rebuked by Christ because they acted in a manner opposite to the message of their preaching, an image of hypocrisy he applied equally to negligent curial prelates and parish priests. In Clamanges' view, mendicants were greedy and deceitful, acting like two-faced hypocrites and rapacious wolves. Using an even stronger accusation, he compared them to the priests of Baal who acted in an adulterous manner and even engaged in sexual encounters with the young. Canons of cathedral chapters, meanwhile, sired illegitimate children with prostitutes and lived carnal lives as Epicurean pigs. They conspired to disrupt the peace and stability of the Church by infecting her with the seeds of dissent. Canons exploited their clerical immunity to cheat everyone: God, the Church, and particularly the poor who had no place of appeal.[5]

Clamanges often portrayed his greatest fear—that the Church was in mortal danger—by adapting classical and patristic images to describe her as a ship floundering in stormy seas.[6] In concluding *De ruina*, he

5. Coville, *Le Traité*, 135–42, especially at 142: *"Nam quid, obsecro, aliud sunt hoc tempore puellarum monasteria, nisi quedam non dico Deo sanctuaria, sed Veneris execranda prostibula, sed lascivorum et impudicorum juvenum ad libidines explendas receptacula, ut idem sit hodie puellam velare quod ad publice scortandum exponere."*

6. In early catechesis the Church was often depicted as a ship, as by Justin Martyr and Tertullian; Origen and Cyprian identified the Church/ship as the place of salvation. An Old Testament precedent of a ship as a place of safety amid stormy seas is the story of Noah's ark (Gn 6:11–8:22). See *New Catholic Encyclopedia* 13:867, s.v. "symbolism, early Christian." For the iconography of the Church as a ship, see *Lexikon der Christlichen Ikonographie* 4:61–67, s.v. "Schiff"; on the Church more particularly as the ship of Peter, see 8:158–74, s.v. "Petrus Apostel, Bischof von Rom."

described the times as full of tempests: the Church was a ship tossed about seeking a safe port. He likened the tax collectors from Avignon's apostolic camera to Charybdis, from whom no one escaped: the Gallican Church, full of scandal, was battered between Scylla and Charybdis. To Charles VI he described the Church as a ship beset continually by tempests and shaken by pride so that she could scarcely hold herself together: Scylla, Charbydis, and Cerberus all threatened to tear her apart and devour her. Even the songs of the Sirens conspired to lull those in the Church to sleep.[7] Clamanges sometimes enhanced this imagery with the New Testament story of Jesus calming the waters, as in one letter where he suggested all in the Church should strenuously cry out to God for help, just as the disciples called out to Jesus to save them in the storm at sea. He did not suggest so drastic a plea in his letter to Charles VI, however, suggesting only that the sleeping rulers of the Church should be roused to action so the faithful would receive proper care. Or, Clamanges asked the king with bald sarcasm, should they just let the rectors sleep and allow the ship to be deluged?[8]

Clamanges used other images besides the Church as a battered ship to emphasize her division and wounds. He discussed the Schism by recounting how the twelve tribes of ancient Israel had divided into the northern and southern kingdoms, thereby exposing themselves to attack and eventually to the Babylonian captivity. Clamanges warned at the conclusion of *De ruina* that the same kind of fate was to be feared for the Church because the Schism repeated this grave error. He recalled the division and destruction which had led to the Babylonian captivity near the end of *Contra prelatos symoniacos* a decade later to reiterate the need for reform and concord.[9] In one of the final chapters of *De ruina,* he described the Church as a long-neglected body that required a doctor's care. The Church's divided and sick parts barely held together any longer: her body was unhealthy from head to foot. Likewise, in one of his letters to the general council at Constance about fifteen years later,

7. Coville, *Le Traité,* 155, 120, 150; C 2.25–3.31, 3.53–55 (L 2:3). Clamanges wrote in much the same terms in a 1398 letter to Gerson from Langres: C 98.29–37 (L 2:60).

8. C 605.140–43 (L 2:250); C 4.72–93 (L 2:4). The storm at sea is found in Mt 8:23–26, Mk 4:35–39, Lk 8:22–24; Old Testament precedents of God's power over the stormy seas are Pss 65:8, 89:10, 106:9, 107:28–30.

9. Coville, *Le Traité,* 153–54; B 2:147.333–148.336 (L 1:165).

Clamanges described the Schism as an old, sharp wound that was difficult to cure. In his poem *Deploratio calamitatis ecclesiastice,* Clamanges
combined historical precedents of troubled kingdoms with the image of
a sick body. He pointed out that the fall of the Roman Empire was due
not so much to outside assault as to sedition from within. He then drew
an important lesson for the Church: internal trouble, such as in the
heart, robs the body of life.[10]

However pessimistic this imagery, there was also an important element of optimism complementing Clamanges' criticisms. He did not
use the imagery of a floundering ship only in a negative way, for
instance. A number of passages focused not so much on the dangers of
the stormy seas as on the promise of a safe port. Peter's ship could be
tossed and agitated by a wild storm but not sunk, Clamanges promised
Charles VI. In *De fructu heremi,* he noted that while the devil threatens
to shipwreck people who are looking for a safe port, divine mercy calls
them back from errors. Though this world was a sea full of troubles and
the danger of shipwreck, he wrote elsewhere, the faithful's home was
above this world. That heavenly home would be a life of eternal happiness and peace—if the faithful navigated through the present world with
vigilance and always aspired to the higher world.[11] As the Schism and
immorality wore on, Clamanges reminded his correspondents that at
least some would survive the storm of sin and the torrent of vices to
avoid the danger of shipwreck and reach the port of eternal salvation.
There was cause for hope: Jesus had come to heal sinners by preaching
righteousness in a world as stained by sin and crime as it had been in the
Old Testament, when Israel's once snow-white leaders had been black-
ened by deformed ways. Christians of their own era were just as guilty of
many sins, but Christ had come precisely to save the lost sheep of Israel.
Though the times were as terrible as they had been in the past, there was
still a chance to be saved. As the Church suffered, many were being purified.[12]

10. Coville, *Le Traité,* 153, following Is 1:6; C 551.41–43 (L 2:310); C 647.62–73, 83–87
(Coville, *Recherches,* 262.59–263.70, 263.80–84).

11. C 110.345–47 (L 2:67); B 2:37.324–29 (L 1:127); C 593.49–54 (L 2:243).

12. C 342.75–343.111 (L 2:210); C 348.15–39 (L 2:213), following Lam 4:7–8, Mt 15:24; C
354.258–355.281 (L 2:217).

GOD AND MAN: THE HUMANISM
OF REFORM

Clamanges' faith in humanity's ability to respond to the urgent need for reform in the troubled Church built upon patristic and medieval reform traditions. He was particularly indebted to their fundamental emphases on the dignity and perfectibility of the human condition as well as on the possibilities of man's reforming himself in partnership with God.

Gerhart B. Ladner demonstrated that in their reform ideology the Fathers primarily built upon an optimistic conception of human nature. The earliest Christian idea of reform sought a personal or individual reform through which man tried to reclaim the image and likeness of God in which he had been created (Gn 1:26), but had lost in Adam's fall. Paul particularly demonstrated in his epistles that man's efforts at spiritual regeneration would produce a reformation of his image and likeness of God (2 Cor 3:18, Col 3:10). The Greek Fathers, among them Origen, contended that at the end of time, man would be restored to the original bliss of the garden that he had enjoyed before Adam's fall. Clamanges did not closely follow the Greek Fathers, however. Their particular emphasis on the recovery of the lost *imago Dei* does not appear in Clamanges' writings in those familiar terms, nor does Clamanges consistently adhere to their common calls for complete withdrawal from the world. Clamanges did, of course, have his own years of retreat, but those he considered active exiles. Indeed, no one involved in the Schism and working as a papal secretary or university *magister* could conceive of reform in Gregory of Nyssa's purely spiritual terms.

Patristic ideas of reform and mankind's restoration did not discuss a simple return to a pre-fallen state, however. Paul and Tertullian among others believed man's reform would result in a condition beyond his original garden state. This concept of a *reformatio in melius* developed especially in the West and distinguishes the Latin from the Greek Fathers. The western idea was that Christians would receive a fuller measure of grace than Adam had enjoyed in the garden because Christ had come after Adam. Rebirth in Christ by baptism represented a greater birth than Adam's creation: man would not only return to paradise but attain a state beyond Adam's. The idea of a *reformatio in melius* received its most extensive treatment from Augustine, who held man's renewal would surpass Adam's original state to entail a spiritual state that Adam would have received had he not fallen. But Augustine noted the fullness of this spiritual state, which can be renewed in the present life, will only be completely achieved in the next life. The final result of mankind's restoration would be a deification, albeit inferior to Christ's nature, by grace and adoption.

Man's reform in the image of God would ultimately be accomplished by God and not man. This conception, however, did not resign the Fathers to a description of humans as completely ineffective actors who should not even make the effort to reform. As Ladner put it in his well-known definition, for the Fathers reform was "the idea of free, intentional and ever perfectible, multiple, prolonged and ever repeated efforts by man to reassert and augment values pre-existent in the spiritual-material compound of the world." Indeed, the Fathers implicitly treated a partnership between humanity and divinity that Clamanges would emphasize explicitly in his own writings on reform. Clamanges stressed personal reform was a process marked by intentional, repeated effort and penance. These were key aspects of personal reform in the Latin Fathers' ideas of reform, building on the Pauline depiction of spiritual progress as a process of continual human action and sanctification with the Holy Spirit's aid. In the western mind, this process was particularly accomplished through the imitation of Christ, especially in his suffering. Purgation and the imitation of Christ emerged as central to Clamanges' ideas of *reformatio personalis,* following the tradition of the Latin Fathers.[13]

The Fathers' primary, optimistic idea of the perfectible state of humanity was inherited by those scholars who established scholastic humanism as a central aspect of the twelfth century Renaissance. In the twelfth and thirteenth centuries, scholastic humanists resurrected the idea men could restore themselves, with divine aid, to a garden-like state of knowledge. This process of recovery had been at work since the fall

13. Ladner, *The Idea of Reform,* passim, with quotation at 35; see also Eugenio Garin, "La *'Dignitas hominis'* e la letteratura patristica," *Rinascita* 4 (1938): 102–46.

and flood via the prophets and Greco-Roman insights into human nature, but it had ceased with the Roman Empire's collapse. About 1050, the recovery was resumed through the editing of texts which had survived the intervening centuries since Rome fell. This endeavor was an optimistic one that was part of the high medieval "sense of enlargement," to use R. W. Southern's phrase, in political, social, economic, and intellectual fields. This exercise was not simply academic but also personal and pastoral: scholastic humanists aimed not only to systematize Christian doctrine, but also to apply dogma to Christian conduct and spread their teachings through sermons, manuals, and handbooks for pastors.

Several characteristic features of medieval scholastic humanism informed Clamanges' reform thought. First, scholastic humanism embraced the supernatural, but not to the detriment of human capabilities. God was seen as being ultimately responsible for helping mankind, but men were to seize the many aids God offered to exercise their great potentiality and to return to their pre-fallen state of knowledge and grace. Second, scholastic humanism embraced the key patristic idea of the dignity of human nature. Men were fallen, but scholastic humanists were optimistic about the chances for recovering as much knowledge as was possible given their fallen state. Third, men's knowledge of God would come from knowledge of themselves. This introspective approach actually grew from monastic roots whereby a monk would look within himself in order to learn to look beyond himself. Clamanges placed a high value on each man's personal growth as a prerequisite for pastoral reform, even though in his era the sense of enlargement from the twelfth and thirteenth centuries had dissipated considerably. The fourteenth and fifteenth centuries ushered in an age of considerable disorder: wars, social revolts, heresies, the Schism, plagues and droughts that brought depopulation, and a general reversal of the economic and territorial expansion that had marked the previous two centuries. In Southern's understated words, optimism and the sense of enlargement were replaced by "the depressing sense that nothing was going well."[14]

14. Robert L. Benson and Giles Constable, with Carol D. Lanham, eds., *Renaissance and Renewal in the Twelfth Century* (Cambridge: Harvard University Press, 1982); M.-D. Chenu, *La théologie au douzième siècle* (Paris: J. Vrin, 1957). The present summary of

Clamanges was the late medieval heir of patristic and high medieval humanists who centered on personal growth and pastoral service as much as he was a "Renaissance" or literary humanist concerned with linguistic style. Further evidence for the kind of spiritual humanism that imbued the content of Clamanges' reform thought comes from Paul Oskar Kristeller and Charles Trinkaus. Literary scholars typically highlight linguistic aspects of medieval humanists, but Kristeller and Trinkaus also perceive in their elegant writings a deep sensitivity to patristic and medieval traditions concerning the state of man. For many humanists of Clamanges' era, man's dignity comes from God and rests in his free ability to choose wisely for good (although he is able to choose otherwise); to accept the duty to lead a morally correct life; and to fulfill his human potential. The inherent optimism in this portrait of man focused on the idea that humanity and divinity acted in partnership. Late medieval humanists picked up the core reform scenario treated by the Fathers: man was made in the image and likeness of God, fell with Adam's sin, was redeemed by Christ's incarnation and resurrection, and has been trying to improve his condition by striving for divinity ever since. In this schema, man did not act passively but was, in Trinkaus' description, "alive, actively assertive, cunningly designing, storming the gates of heaven." Since human potential was tied to divine providence, the exercise of human potential was not the exaltation of man over God, but the glorification of the divinity which had created humanity. Man's free will was an essential aspect of his striving to connect with his innate divinity, an approach Trinkaus identified as an "anthropocentric theology" based on a revival of interest in the Fathers.[15]

---

scholastic humanism follows R. W. Southern, *Scholastic Humanism and the Unification of Europe,* vol. 1, *Foundations* (Oxford: Basil Blackwell, 1995), 1–57, and *Medieval Humanism and Other Studies* (Oxford: Basil Blackwell, 1970), 29–60.

15. Paul Oskar Kristeller, *Renaissance Thought and Its Sources,* ed. Michael Moony (New York: Columbia University Press, 1979), especially 169–96. Charles Trinkaus, *In Our Image and Likeness: Humanity and Divinity in Italian Humanist Thought,* 2 vols. (Chicago: University of Chicago Press, 1970), especially 1:xiv–xxiv and 2:761–74. The scholarship on literary humanism in France is extensive. See especially Gilbert Ouy, "Paris, l'un des principaux foyers de l'humanisme en Europe au début du XVe siècle," *Bulletin de la société de l'histoire de Paris et de l'Île-de-France* (1967–68): 71–98, and "Le collège de Navarre, berceau de l'humanisme française," *Actes du 95e congrès national des sociétés savantes, Reims 1970. Section de philologie et d'histoire jusqu'à 1610,* vol. 1, *Enseignement et vie intellectuelle (IXe–XVIe*

Clamanges at times directly appealed to God for help and emphasized man's failures, leaving the initial impression he saw divine action as
the only way to reform the Church. Much of his poem *Deploratio
calamitatis ecclesiastice* was an appeal to Christ and the Father to turn
their attentions to the afflicted Church. In *De ruina,* Clamanges stressed
God's efforts to help the Church and indicated a certain divine disdain
for human attempts at reform. It is not the work of man to resolve the
Schism because only God, as doctor, can heal this particular wound.
Man's efforts only made matters worse. God, in fact, laughs at men who
think they are able to solve the Church's problems by their own clever
efforts without divine aid. Consistent with the exasperated, almost
despairing tone of *De ruina,* Clamanges ended not with an exhortation
for human action but with a desperate plea for Jesus to look with mercy
and leniency upon the many examples of human sin and error that mer-
ited a fierce retribution.[16]

As he watched the papal curia in Avignon a few years earlier, Clamanges had contrasted the weaknesses of human infirmity with God's
gifts, which alone make men strong and grant them virtue. Men are like
leaves blown in the wind while God is the source of strength, he reminded Gerson. Because of this situation, Clamanges frequently underscored
the need for divine aid: man's futile and unworthy efforts must be
restricted to pious prayers that God protect and reform His interests.[17]
Unless Christ acted quickly, the Schism and other wounds would plunge

---

siècle) (Paris: Bibliothèque Nationale, 1975): 275–99; G. Matteo Roccati, "La formation des
humanistes dans le dernier quart du XIV siècle," in *Pratiques de la culture écrite en France
au XVe siècle,* ed. Monique Ornato and Nicole Pons (Louvain-la-Neuve: Fédération Internationale des Instituts d'Études Médiévales, 1995), 55–73, and "La formazione intellettuale
di Jean Gerson (1363–1429): Un esempio del rinnovamento umanistico degli studi," in
L'educazione e la formazione intellettuale nell'età dell'umanesimo, ed. Luisa Rotondi Secchi
Tarugi (Milan: Guerini e Associati, 1992), 229–44; Dario Cecchetti, *L'evoluzione del latino
umanistico in Francia* (Paris: Éditions CEMI, 1986).

16. Coville, *Le Traité,* 151–52, 155–56.

17. C 65.73–83 (L 2:41), following Pss 28:8, 60:14, 75:4, 118:14; Ex 15:2; Is 12:2. Mark S.
Burrows argues that, after Constance, Gerson assigned to God alone the task of reforming
the Church because the Hussites persisted even though Jan Hus had been excommunicated and executed in 1415. This fact caused Gerson to emphasize men could only pray for
God to act: Burrows, *Jean Gerson and De Consolatione Theologiae (1418): The Consolation of
a Biblical and Reforming Theology for a Disordered Age* (Tübingen: J. C. B. Mohr [Paul
Siebeck], 1991), 259.

the Church into the depths of misery, Clamanges told Benedict XIII. Employing a litany of scriptural citations, Clamanges appealed to Jesus to return His eyes to His spouse the Church to remove her stain, poison, and worthlessness; to free her from imminent ruin and destruction; and to purge His temple, a house of prayer that had been turned into a den of thieves.[18] He dramatically placed a similar plea for divine intervention into the metaphoric mouth of the Church herself in another letter. She begged her spouse to remember His promise to be with her until the end of the world and concluded with a series of petitions asking Christ to rescue her from so many troubles. Clamanges similarly concluded *Contra prelatos symoniacos* with a direct request for Christ to see how badly His spouse, whom He had redeemed with His blood, had been stained and ruined. There he called upon Christ to heal the Church by using the vegetative reform imagery of God separating the wheat from the chaff and caring for a vineyard.[19]

Clamanges told Benedict XIII that ultimately the current state of the Church would not be improved by human efforts. Only God's holy arm could save His sheep from disorder, restore the terrible collapse of the Church, and bring back her pristine honor and dignity. Even to the Constance delegates, Clamanges could stress divine action. It was true men had already worked for long periods of time by using human counsel, thinking, and advice. They had convened together and consulted to seek peace, to treat subtle arguments, and to attempt many tasks and remedies. But no benefit was produced for the terrible disease that beset the Church; in fact, man's labors only made matters more tangled and confused. The way to end the sickness caused by greed and division would be to satiate God's anger, just as a doctor can only cure a body of

18. C 82.17–83.25 (L 2:51); C 90:275–94 (L 2:55), following Ps 119:49–50, Mt 28:20, 1 Pt 2:5–6, Is 56:7, Jer 7:11, Mt 21:13, Mk 11:17, Lk 19:46, Ps 80:15–16. Note the direct address, even command, to Christ throughout, especially at ll. 275–79, 288–89: *"Respice, benignissime Ihesu, pia compassione sponsam tuam tamque horrendam ab illa maculam, tantum virus, tantam nequitiam velociter repelle. Retorque ad illam oculos tuos, si forte offensus eos avertisti . . . ab imminente ruina ac demolitione libera. . . ."*

19. C 117.605–118.644 (L 2:71–72); B 2:148.341–43 (L 1:166), following Jer 15:7, Mt 3:12, Lk 3:17, Is 5:1–2, 4. Clamanges elsewhere asked God to spare His people by pruning, watering, and fertilizing them: C 91.312–29 (L 2:55–56). In *De ruina*, he used the imagery of a once-fertile garden that was now overrun and barren in another direct request for divine aid: Coville, *Le Traité,* 143.

illness by removing its source. Clamanges reminded the delegates that in order to remove greed and division they must rely on God's correction and aid, not on human hope, the subtleties of human knowledge, or men's fancy speeches and arguments. Without the Spirit's aid, these actions would prove fruitless.[20]

It may seem Clamanges left the act of reform entirely to God, but closer examination reveals a humanistic symbiosis between the roles of God and man in reforming the Church. While Clamanges acknowledged God cares for His flock and saves His sheep, he also identified man's duty to call for God's help and to accept divine aid in working for reform. For Clamanges, healing the Church was an act of partnership between God and man based on the patristic and medieval traditions of the humanism of reform.

As frequently as Clamanges urged men to rely on God, he encouraged them to hasten to the work of reform themselves. Clamanges reminded d'Ailly the opportunity to confound or to help the Church was in his hands: he could choose to act for the good of the Church or for further treachery. If men acted for good, there would be no problems; if they acted for ill, there would be only more troubles and no hope for the Church. Although in *De fructu heremi* he cited Paul's admonition that men must not take credit for their actions but remember all comes from God, Clamanges went well beyond the almost complete reliance on divine grace he exhibited elsewhere. In contrast, he seized the opportunity offered by God's gifts to rouse men to action. They must accept divine aid and get to work without making excuses that the times are wicked, their bodies are weak, or they are ignorant. Men could freely choose to be lazy and sluggish, but they should act with God's aid. His cajoling tone and prods to cooperate with divine help were repeated in a letter to theology students at the Collège de Navarre. With a sharp rhetorical rebuke, Clamanges asked his correspondents whether men should be admired when they persisted in a torrent of vices and crimes despite heavenly aid.[21]

---

20. C 93.375–84 (L 2:56–57), following Ps 98:1; C 489.83–91, 94–101 (L 2:291–92); C 551.54–552.70 (L 1:311), following Jb 5:18; Wis 9:14; Pss 13:2, 74:19, 98:1; Mt 28:20.
21. C 178.130–179.140 (L 2:106); B 2:33.213–34.221 (L 1:125), following 2 Cor 3:5; C 387.11–19 (L 2:230).

Clamanges emphasized man's active response to God's help to Charles VI and Benedict XIII. The king should not fear the difficult work ahead because the task would be rendered easier with God's help. After promising Charles VI that Jesus would offer virtue, peace, and honor with other graces, Clamanges stressed Christ directed the efforts of those who served Him. He informed the king that the greatest dignity of man came from serving God and helping divine action as God's aide and ally. There was also no need for Benedict XIII to fear: instead of deserting his servant, Christ would promote the curing and reforming of the sick Church by guiding Benedict and protecting him from enemies. Unlike other letters that Clamanges concluded with a reminder to rely on divine aid, this one to Benedict XIII ended with a call for the pope to gather together zealous and faithful men—and to get to work.[22]

Clamanges explained the alliance between humanity and divinity to Jean de Montreuil during his first active exile. He told his close friend God's role was to bring mankind to a better life through purgation, but it was man's task to respond to this heavenly gift by acting correctly and justly. Enlightened by study, men should earn the merits of heaven and avoid hell by zealous living and good works. His call for human action in reform was also reflected in several undated letters to Nicolas de Baye. God stands at man's door and knocks, rousing men from their sleep as Christ raised Lazarus. Men should respond to this knock because it was better to take up the light yoke of Christ and to serve God through many pious works than to serve man. God favored action and not inactivity in men. Stirred by the fire of the Holy Spirit, men should be unwilling to permit delay or to slide back. God preferred the diligent and the active, spitting from His mouth the fretful or those who were lukewarm in their sentiments and actions. Clamanges also told his friend men should choose to live as sons of God. The Father would teach and correct His sons; then they would understand the heavenly patrimony given to them because they were made in the image of God's Son. Men should strive with good actions to placate divine wrath; to be made worthy of divine grace; to endure with patience the justice due to them for their sins; to amend their conduct; and to conquer evil with good. They

22. C 5:127–29 (L 2:5); C 6:135–39, 141–46, 156–59 (L 2:5), following 1 Cor 3:9; C 14.260–15.285 (L 2:10).

must convert themselves to divine service and be reconciled with God. Clamanges stressed it was incumbent upon men to act by seeking the Lord humbly with perseverance, love, hope, freedom, and vigilance. They should plead and pray devoutly for divine aid in the knowledge that with God's help they would continue to improve and perfect themselves.[23]

Clamanges forcefully applied this theme of human action in a 1416 letter sent to delegates attending the general council at Constance. Breaking from his prior reliance on divine action at Constance, he spurred the delegates to innovative efforts. Filled with the purifying grace of God, they should not be broken by adversity, grow lukewarm, permit delay, or leave the glorious tasks of God uncompleted. Nothing should be judged useful that would get in the delegates' way, and nothing should be judged useless that would help them achieve their goals. Clamanges went beyond encouragement and was bluntly pragmatic near the end of this letter. He urged them to work hard toward a resolution of the Church's troubles by being flexible and open to a number of possible solutions. If one way fails, they should try another to resolve the areas in dispute. Unlike Isaac, who had only one blessing to give to his sons Jacob and Esau, the Church had many ways to heal herself. All of these ways should be pursued just as a doctor has many remedies he can try when any one is not effective.

Clamanges used two classical references to illustrate his point. First, he cited a line from *The Lady of Andros* by the Roman playwright Terence to tell the delegates that if what someone wants to do is not possible, then he ought to wish for what is possible. Second, Clamanges referred to the *Nicomachean Ethics* of Aristotle where the Greek philosopher discussed the principle of *epikeia,* that is, equity. The word *epikeia* was used by Aristotle to describe how a particular law binding a republic ought to be adapted so its original spirit may correctly be applied to circumstances other than those within which the law had originally been

23. C 140.18–141.23, 141.37–44 (L 2:84); C 593.62–594.87 (L 2:244), following Rv 3:15–16 and 20, Jn 11:11, Mt 11:29–30; C 603.84–100 (L 2:249), following Rom 8:29 and 12:21, Mal 3:7, Zec 1:3; C 603.104–605.140 (L 2:249–50). The message that men are helped by divine grace to do good, to avoid giving offense to God, and to achieve heaven was also the theme of a letter to a Parisian theology student about 1417: C 633.45–71 (L 2:346–47).

conceived. Clamanges used Aristotle's notion of *epikeia* to explain why in certain special situations only indefinite rules should be applied, as in the philosopher's example of the Lesbian builders who used a flexible lead ruler to guide molding in stonework, to which he contrasted the iron and unbending rules that governed the Spartans. Delegates at Constance, Clamanges advised, must in the end not stand on rigid principle but act flexibly, reasonably, and charitably for good and justice.[24]

CLAMANGES ON HIS OWN TASK

Clamanges worked at the University of Paris and in the Avignon curia, yet he preferred to exhort others to participate in the events of their day and to give them advice on how to do so. His role in encouraging action has been seen in letters that entreated his readers to understand the partnership between human action and divine aid, which allowed men to take up the task of reform. When his entire career is taken into consideration—his periods of public service and active exile—this strong background role emerges as the principal characteristic of Clamanges' self-defined task as reformer.

Clamanges identified his own task, which he exercised most frequently behind the scenes, as a personal duty and a professional burden. The gentlest discussion of his motivations for writing on reform comes from a letter to Nicolas de Baye, written from Fontaine-au-Bois during his second active exile. There Clamanges offered a long exposition of his love for writing letters, especially to friends. Letters provided mutual support, consolation, and nourishment. Nothing hard or rigid ought to be said among friends. Correspondents should raise each other's spirits, telling the truth in a way that did not point out errors for condemnation as much as display them for correction. It is better to speak in a pleasing

24. C 554.140–58 (L 2:312), following Lk 1:79, Jn 11:52; C 555.210–557.261 (L 2:313–14), following Gn 27:38. For the quotation from Terence, see John Sargeaunt, trans., *Terence*, 2 vols. (Cambridge: Harvard University Press, 1953), 1:32–33. For the reference to Aristotle, see H. Rackham, trans., *Aristotle: The Nicomachean Ethics* (Cambridge: Harvard University Press, 1945), 316–17 [V.x.7–8]. The principle of *epikeia* was key to much of Gerson's reform thought. He specifically applied it to resolving the highly extraordinary situation of the Schism, noting that only spiritual men and theologians who were moral and trained in Scripture could know when and how to apply the principle: Pascoe, *Jean Gerson*, 65–78, 94–99.

way as the poets do or else no positive end would result. However, Clamanges reiterated significantly, truth must always stand behind delightful words: if friends covered the truth with lies, how could they receive the help they required? There was no point in writing unless to show the light of truth simply and plainly to friends. Later in this letter Clamanges turned to a series of scriptural citations to exhort the continued correction of errors in truth and fraternal charity; to stress that friends bear each other's burdens; and to cajole his correspondent to point out transgressions in a spirit of leniency instead of harshness. Clamanges told delegates at Constance that any truth he wrote to them originated not with himself but had been drawn from Scripture and inspired by the Holy Spirit which was, according to Ambrose and Augustine, the source of all truth. Clamanges asserted that if he spoke the truth it was only because God who alone is truth was speaking through him.[25]

Clamanges also considered his role as reformer a professional burden that he had to fulfill harshly, as his fierce criticisms of the Church in *De ruina* attest. In *De studio theologico,* he declared he wrote to instruct raw recruits who, as future soldiers of Christ, needed to be trained and tested. In letters to Benedict XIII and Gerson, he explicated the parable of the talents to portray himself as a servant during difficult times emulating the model of classical orators.[26] Clamanges also turned to the orator's professional duty in a 1395 letter to unnamed friends who objected to the sharp tone of correction he had used toward Benedict XIII the previous year. Clamanges explained he had written boldly to the Avignon pope because of his duty as a learned person to point out errors skillfully so they could be corrected. He must not only indicate behavior that should be amended, but also spur people to take action, even if that meant provoking ire or giving offense. Clamanges admitted he might have fulfilled

---

25. C 462.20–463.31 (L 2:276); C 463.46–464.81 (L 2:276–77); C 465.148–466.179 (L 2:278), following 1 Cor 13:7, Col 3:13, Gal 6:1–2, Rom 11:20, Wis 1:6, 1 Cor 4:20; C 526.32–35 (L 1:65), 526.46–527.56 (L 1:65–66), following Jn 14:17, 15:26, 16:13, and 1 Jn 4:6. Clamanges referred here to Ambrose's commentary on 1 Cor 12:3, *"sed spiritus sancti veritate profusum est. quicquid enim verum a quocumque dicitur, a sancto dicitur spiritu"*: CSEL 81/2, 132. He also quoted Augustine's *Letter 238* to the Arian Pascentius following Rom 3:4: *"neque enim in nobis ipsis, vel per nos ipsos veraces sumus cum sumus; sed cum ille in servis suis loquitur, qui solus est verax"*: PL 33:1041.

26. B 2:104.13–14 (d'Achery, 1:473); Bernstein, NP, 7–10.

his duty to Benedict XIII in an inconsiderate, imprudent, inept, or unadorned manner. But he asked his readers to concede his attempt was praiseworthy because, as among friends, it was better to speak the truth in an inelegant or uncultured way than to offer ornate and cloaked lies.

Elsewhere Clamanges attributed his task of calling for reform both gently and harshly to his love for the Church. He explained to Benedict XIII he had dared to enter into error or to move away from the truth through ignorance because of his commitment to the Church. He was driven not by blind or evil emotions, worldly ambition, or personal hatred, but by a most sincere zeal for reforming the Church peacefully and agreeably. He assured the delegates at Constance he wrote nothing except what was for the good of the Church. He then asked his friends there to correct him if he had made any errors or had asserted any points that should be argued or doubted. Practicing what he had preached in other letters to friends, Clamanges added he had written strongly to expose scandals and to admonish the faithful so errors could be corrected. But, he wrote in defense of his comments, he did not think any errors or doubtful statements that he might have made should be imputed to temerity on his part.[27]

Clamanges' burden to encourage others especially targeted d'Ailly and Gerson, whom he considered better able to effect the reforms he suggested. Several times Clamanges demonstrated the high regard with which he held d'Ailly, his friend and mentor from his first years at the Collège de Navarre. In *De ruina,* after lengthy complaints about prelates and clerics of varying ranks, Clamanges paused to mention he did not include d'Ailly among those he censured. In contrast to his fellow bishops, d'Ailly rose from among their cloudy tempests like a rose amid thorns or a precious gem among the cheapest stones. When Clamanges urged Benedict XIII to gather together faithful, zealous, learned, moral, and wise men who would not spurn the work of the Church nor deceive the pope, he singled out only d'Ailly by name. He also praised d'Ailly directly: in a letter written when both were exiled from Paris because of their opposition to the 1398–1403 withdrawal of obedience, Clamanges

27. C 16.31–17.66 (L 2:11–12); C 18.97–107 (L 2:12); C 26.407–11 (L 2:17); C 84.86–94 (L 2:52); C 547.772–85 (L 1:77).

told d'Ailly he could find more and better remedies for the Church's wounds than Clamanges himself. If d'Ailly discovered any, he should not hide them but offer the remedies to Clamanges and others who were suffering, so that together they could work their way out of the great danger. He later declared d'Ailly was among the most illustrious men in the world and did not deserve to be attacked amid the arguments about the Schism.[28]

Clamanges also held in high regard his contemporary, Gerson, a fellow protégé of d'Ailly. Writing in 1405 or 1406 from Nice, Clamanges with compassion told Gerson he suffered without cause or blame more than Clamanges did. Several years later, Clamanges maintained he could not offer any advice to his friend. He began by telling Gerson his letters comforted him: Gerson instructed and exhorted Clamanges with very useful, healthy advice on how to live according to God's will. Clamanges then spent the rest of this letter discussing how men grow from their difficulties, but concluded by denying to himself the role of Gerson's teacher. He could not teach anything to Gerson, whom he likened to Minerva, the Roman goddess of wisdom, but he had written to tell others what actions should be taken or avoided.[29]

Clamanges' observations about d'Ailly and Gerson reveal important insights concerning how he saw his own task behind the scenes compared with theirs. While his statements that they were inherently better men than he can be formulaic, this does not mitigate Clamanges' genuine respect for his friends. But beyond this familiar ode to colleagues, he made a more trenchant point: d'Ailly and Gerson could influence reform more directly and effectively because of their status as church statesmen. They had higher connections, exercised more influence, and were better suited for negotiations within the upper echelons of ecclesiastical and civil politics. In a letter written during the 1398–1403 withdrawal, Clamanges pressed Gerson to inform the princes of the troubles being visited upon the Church, including the loss of her dignity and liberty. Gerson could open the eyes of those princes who were blinded by

28. Coville, *Le Traité*, 144; C 14.265–15.285 (L 2:10); C 176.34–40 (L 2:105); C 220.91–99 (L 2:134–35).
29. C 208.21–24 (L 2:127); C 286.3–6 (L 2:177); C 290.146–49 (L 2:179).

ambition to their own ruin. He should dissuade them from actions that fouled ecclesiastical dignity, led them to evil, and allowed dangers to persist. Through his preaching, Clamanges asserted, Gerson could say all of this to the princes with more eloquence and ardor than Clamanges' own letter, making the message more efficacious.[30]

Clamanges was not, however, without his criticisms of how d'Ailly and Gerson responded to the tasks of reform he set before them. He noted in his friends a tendency toward cautious moderation and too much patience; in response, he often gently exhorted or even chided them to take more decisive action. His impatience and amicable criticism come through in a letter to Gerson from early 1398, before the withdrawal was approved. He encouraged his friend to take action in Paris to prevent the forces for withdrawal that were gaining ground. Because great trouble in the Church was not being addressed and remedies were being blocked, the task of helping the Church fell to them; they should act, at least by praying to God. But in his next breath Clamanges went further: while he did not deny the importance of prayer, at this crucial moment of the Schism Clamanges wanted action besides prayer. Patience, Clamanges continued, would not work in the current circumstances and might be foolish. Although in private matters it may be praiseworthy to act patiently, in the matter of injury to God and the Church worthy men must not be muted by silent patience but move with a zealous, generous spirit to resist wicked efforts. Though Christ was patient, even He reached a point where He acted physically to drive out the moneychangers from the Temple: whose example was more effective in approving the taking of action than Christ's?[31]

30. C 184.146–185.182 (L 2:110). Lamenting that virtuous men acting to reform the Church had come under criticism, Clamanges included d'Ailly among them but pointedly excluded himself in 1408: C 220.80–85 (L 2:134): *"Nec ista quidem tam propter me dixerim, qui nichil egregium gessi, quam propter te et alios multos magna virtute decorates, quorum comparatione nichil verius sum, qui nullam adhuc expressam virtutis imaginem, sed nudam ac tenuem umbram vix attigi."* Anton Simon rightly identified Clamanges as earnest and frustrated, not indifferent, as he cajoled others to act: *Studien zu Nikolaus von Clemanges* (Endingen: Druck von Emil Wild, 1929), 106–108.

31. C 63.11–29 (L 2:40–41); C 64.34–38, 59–67 (L 2:41); C 65.83–96 (L 2:41–42), following Mt 21:12–13, Mk 11:15–17, Lk 19:45–46, Jn 2:13–16. Bernstein placed this letter in the broader context of the duty of the eloquent man to serve the Church or state especially during crisis: NP, 9–10.

Clamanges most boldly discharged his self-assigned role as gadfly when writing to Charles VI and Benedict XIII. His letters to Charles VI in 1394 and 1402 shared a central goal: to goad the king into taking up the tasks of uniting and reforming the Church. How better and more acceptably could Charles VI serve the Church than to free her from trouble? Clamanges said he dared to write because the situation was so bad and there were many calamities. In closing, he told Charles VI he had spoken in a forward manner so the king would clearly see the great abyss of damnation and plague affecting the Church. He should not be deceived by men who tried to disturb and impede the most sacred peace. Clamanges had good reason to conclude with a defense of his remarks since the rest of the letter was a heavy-handed prod. He laid the effects of the Schism at Charles VI's feet very early on, asking the king how long he would permit the Church to suffer; how long he would allow the holy religion of Christ to be subjected to the mocking and laughter of the unfaithful; and how long he would let the house of God that had been built, consecrated, and dedicated by the seal of Christ's blood be corrupted and demolished. To Charles VI fell the many tasks of healing the weak, aiding the Church beset by injury, watching over the faith, seeking peace, and abolishing the evils of the raging Schism. The French king should be unwilling to neglect the task of protecting the Church, which had been entrusted to him, nor the fame and glory that would come with success. He reminded Charles VI of the French royal family's venerable tradition of protecting the Church: the king should maintain her honor so that he would not defraud the glory of his ancestors, the "most Christian" kings of France.

Clamanges rhetorically put words into the Church's mouth to pressure the king. In a long segment from the 1402 letter, the Church chided Charles for his failure to protect her and then exhorted the king to help now. He was her one hope amid terrible calamities and enemies, but he had let her down and failed to come to her aid. As a result of his idleness, the Church was beset by neglect for Christ, disregard of the faith, and lack of respect for apostolic authority. How had she fallen to such ruin and squalor, having lost her place of respect, honor, and obedience even among Charles VI and other princes? Because all of this distress to the Church and the faith had occurred during his reign, she asked the king whether he was ashamed to be called her son. But after attempting to shame Charles VI into action, Clamanges had the Church take a more positive approach. She instructed him to lead others away from the evil that inflicted her wounds and back to honor, piety, and justice. He must restore freedom to the Church, without which there could be no consolation, health, joy, or good life. The Church then made Charles an enticing promise: if the king's actions in helping the Church did not bring him worldly praise, they would nevertheless bring compassion from Christ at his future judgment.[32]

Clamanges also pushed Benedict XIII to act. He first wrote the Avignon pope in 1394, a move surely intended to catch Benedict's eye. He explained the directness of his comments to the new Avignon pope elected only a few months before, just as he had done with the French king. Clamanges asked Benedict XIII to understand that he dared to write with force only to impel the pope to act quickly. Defending this letter to the friends who objected to its directness, Clamanges declared he would be satisfied if his words had pointed out to Benedict the many vices that needed to be abolished. Clamanges repeated his mandate: he must speak freely or else he would speak falsely and thereby allow faithlessness and perjury to continue. As he would do twenty years later to delegates at Constance, Clamanges challenged his friends to point out any errors in his letter. Since none did, he concluded they must consider his contentions accurate. He conceded he had written to the pope as an equal or an intimate acquaintance, but explained he had done so reverently, moderately, and prudently because individuals in every civil and ecclesiastical rank were subject to correction.[33]

Clamanges exercised his self-assigned role as gadfly to the Avignon pope and the French king with equal intensity, but his letters to Benedict XIII portray a different model of reform leadership than the one he urged on Charles VI when he asked the king to resolve the Schism and

---

32. C 2.7–11, 18–24 (L 2:3); C 5.108–22 (L 2:4); C 6.150–52, 159–65 (L 2:5); C 7.186–91 (L 2:5–6); C 110.353–65 (L 2:67); C 116.560–117.595 (L 2:70–71); C 118.645–119.672 (L 2:72).

33. C 13.232–36 (L 2:9–10); C 15.12–16 (L 2:11); C 22.283–23.304 (L 2:15–16); C 26.411–16 (L 2:17); C 19.163–20.178 (L 2:13); C 22.257–59 (L 2:15).

heal the Church's wounds. Clamanges may have turned to Charles VI
for leadership in 1394 because he had little regard for Clement VII, who
was the Avignon pope when Clamanges wrote to the king that winter. In
that letter, Clamanges described Clement VII as uninterested in protecting the Church and incapable of improving her troubles. He indicted
Clement as a sleeping captain who did not look to the safety of his ship,
blaming him and his crew for the Church's division. Lacking a leader,
the Church was tossed by a storm and threatened by deluge or shipwreck.[34] By contrast, Clamanges later that year confidently invested the
new Avignon pope with the task of leading the reform of the Church.
He described Benedict XIII as Peter's successor, head shepherd, and ship
captain. He must be a good shepherd and watch over his flock, like the
Bethlehem shepherds who kept watch over their sheep when the angels
appeared to them on the night of the Nativity; like Jesus the Good Shepherd; and like Peter to whom Jesus entrusted the care of His flock. Clamanges expressed confidence that Benedict XIII, unlike Clement VII,
could lead the storm-tossed ship of the Church because of his grace,
skill, and power. Other laborers would also work for reform if Benedict
offered a shining, sincere example. There was more burden, labor, and
danger than dignity in the new pope's office, he warned. Hard work was
Benedict XIII's vocation: honor and glory would come from divine service. As one blessed by God, Benedict XIII should rouse himself to his
task of bringing about the peace of the Church, expelling evil and dis-
cord, healing disease, binding wounds, and eliminating the most deadly
plague of the Schism. Clamanges declared the Avignon pope should not
delay or sleep but get to work at once: it was simply impossible for Benedict XIII to be happy while he saw the Church so terribly afflicted.[35]

Clamanges repeated his exhortation for papal leadership in a second
letter to Benedict XIII, this one from the summer of 1398 after he had

34. C 3.33–43, 3.63–4.67, 4.89–93 (L 2:3,4). At C 3.37–38, Clamanges cited Vergil
(*Aeneid,* 6.278) to identify sleep as death's brother, an ominous reference for the Church
led by a sleeping captain.

35. C 8.25–31 (L 2:6); C 9.65–66, 70–74 (L 2:7); C 10.101–6 (L 2:7), following Lk 2:8–9,
Jn 10:11 and 21:17; C 11.129–43 (L 2:8); C 12.169–93 (L 2:8–9); C 13.208–22 (L 2:9), again
noting Clamanges' directness at ll. 211–15: *"Exurge igitur, benedicte Dei, ad opus tuum et ad
opera[t]ionem tuam: affer optatam mundo pacis benedictionem maledictam de Ecclesia discor-
diam expelle, morbum sana, vulnus alliga, pestem virulentissimi schismatis elimina."*

served in the Avignon curia. He reminded the pope he had been given the task of guiding the Church: Benedict XIII's duty was to act with vigilance and navigate the ship to a safe port. Although Clamanges encouraged the king to take the lead early in 1394, four years later he told Benedict the Church should not be anchored in the secular world: the faithful must place their trust in God and not princes, because there would be no salvation among men. He again goaded Benedict XIII to restore the battered ship, which was in danger of being submerged, and to fight the hostility and impediments of her enemies.[36] He emphasized the pope's role as leader in Christ's stead in *Deploratio calamitatis ecclesiastice*. Clamanges first directly addressed Christ as captain, asking Him to navigate the foundering ship of the Church beset by storms and to calm the seas as He had done for His disciples. He then switched from addressing Christ to speaking directly to the pope. Benedict XIII was entrusted with the leadership and care of the ship of the Church by Christ: it was now the pope's responsibility to guard against shipwreck and to protect the crew. If the ship foundered or the crew was harmed, what glory would there be for the pope? Delegated by Jesus and with no time to delay, Clamanges wrote with some impatience, Benedict XIII could not fail to rally men to action and to save the ship because his was the task of Peter, the steersman. He denied delay, rest, or inertia to Benedict XIII. The time for action was now.[37]

Clamanges also took up the call to act "now." In the longer period of his second active exile, he treated more systematically the themes of personal and pastoral reform he had been addressing piecemeal, mostly in letters, during the earlier years of his career. It is to the fruits of his contemplation as they were first developed during Clamanges' earlier career and then nurtured in the more mature years of his second active exile that this study now turns.

36. C 92.349–68 (L 2:56), following Pss 118:8, 146:3. In a letter following Clamanges' break with Benedict XIII, he wrote that an unskilled captain drowns all on his ship with him in turbulent seas. This statement mirrored his 1394 description of Clement VII as a poor ship captain, but Clamanges must be referring here to the stubborn Benedict with whom he had become frustrated: C 362.75–78 (L 2:221).

37. C 647.95–648.132 (Coville, *Recherches*, 263.91–264.129), following Mt 8:23–26, Mk 4:35–39, Lk 8:22–24.

Part II

CHAPTER 3

The Foundation:
Reformatio personalis

An essential patristic theme informs all of Clamanges' comments on the renewal of the late medieval Church: the absolute necessity of personal reform. In order for the institutional Church to overcome her many problems, all of them exacerbated by the Schism, the individual Christian must first undergo a fundamental *reformatio personalis*. Clamanges firmly held that unless each Christian focused on God and returned to spiritual simplicity within, the institutional Church could not be reformed in a lasting, meaningful manner. His inside-out renewal of the Church drew on the prevailing interior, Christocentric piety of his day as well as on the optimistic scholastic humanism that influenced his thought.

For Clamanges, *reformatio personalis* entailed individual spiritual goals best pursued and attained when Christians endeavored to imitate the life of Christ. More specifically for the clergy, each cleric must put aside his personal ambitions and simoniacal dealings, prepare his own heart for the gifts of the Holy Spirit (received in large part from the study of Scripture), and apply himself to the *cura animarum* of his flock in imitation of the good shepherd. Only within this perspective could the Church in the broadest sense return herself to permanent union and peace, putting the Schism, secular entanglements, and worldliness behind her. Personal and institutional reform, of course, are not antithetical for either Clamanges or his contemporaries. Among the many complementary meanings of practical reform Johannes Helmrath identified in medieval councils, the pairing of spiritual and inner reform with institutional and outer reform stands out. Especially for Gerson, inner and institutional reform naturally work dialectically because each Christian is part of the mystical body of Christ.[1]

In terms of emphasis, however, Clamanges more than his confreres concentrated first on the goal of personal reform. His conception of personal reform was a *via purgativa* that the Christian must ground in fear and humility of God, the correcting teacher. Clamanges contended spiritual growth best occurred in solitude, preferably a rural setting away from the politics and distractions of an urban center such as Paris. Thus situated, the Christian could aspire to the fruits of the eremitical life that had instructed and tempered the Old Testament Hebrews, the Fathers, and Christ Himself. These fruits would purge the solitary, prayerful Christian and pave his way to heaven; they would also lead outward to institutional implications.

REFORM THROUGH ADVERSITY

Personal reform could only succeed if Christians accepted a first principle: God repairs and corrects both individuals and the institutional Church by tribulation. It is therefore necessary to understand Clamanges' conception of God as a loving father or teacher who repairs and corrects by purgation. The act of correction by punishment, force, or suffering may at first seem destructive, but it is actually spiritually constructive and edifying, he argued rhetorically in *De prosperitate aduersitatis* and its thematic companion, *De fructu heremi*. Paternal correction and coercion are challenging means to the greater end of purification. He stated clearly in an important, normative theme that the correction of a father is born from love for his children whom he wishes to instruct in order to keep them on the straight path. "Whom I love," Clamanges followed Revelation, "I reprove and chastise." Like a good teacher, God points out errors to lazy students, correcting them for their own discipline and good. While God's demands and chastisement may seem hard,

1. Johannes Helmrath, "Reform als Thema der Konzilien des Spätmittelalters," in *Christian Unity: The Council of Ferrara-Florence 1438/39–1989,* ed. Giuseppe Alberigo (Leuven: Leuven University Press, 1991), 90–95, especially at 93: "Die theologische Verknüpfung von äußerer Mißstandskorrektur und innerer spiritueller Reform, ist auch für das Verständnis des zentralen Zusammenhangs von reformatio capitis und reformatio membrorum wesentlich."

they in fact serve the higher purposes of helping to cleanse men of their impurities and to call their souls to perfection and virtue. Clamanges took some of these ideas from Paul, for whom tribulation, chastisement, and discipline were important keys within the relationship between God the Father and His children. Clamanges applied this Pauline principle to his own ideas on personal reform by way of purgation and correction. He reminded his readers that correction, however harsh, instructs. God offers mercy with His discipline, never leaving His children to suffer alone. Correction is so important it should not be avoided, but even sought out for the good of salvation. With the Psalmist, the Christian should seek to be put to the test. Clamanges fundamentally followed Paul's lesson to the Corinthians and Hebrews: virtue is perfected in infirmity.[2]

Adversity was an important element in an individual's spiritual progress. Clamanges described adversity as a master who teaches in *De filio prodigo*: the prodigal son returns to his father via an inner path of penitence built on his experience of adversity. Although he must be aware of his sins, the prodigal son must not let adversity cause him to despair or allow his sins to stand in the way of his conversion. He must be active: he should go to his father and confess his sins with a heart made humble and contrite by his adversity.[3] Clamanges concentrated on this sincere conversion of heart through adversity as he focused on the moment of the prodigal son's decision to return to his father's house. The prodigal son recognizes he became poor, blind, and sinful when he left his father, and must pursue the task of penitence in three steps related to adversity. First, he must have a contrite heart, represented by his statement, "Father, I have sinned." Second, he must submit to further adversity by asking his father to treat him as one of his paid servants. This act

---

2. B 2:54.213–16 (L 1:136); B 2:60.370 (L 1:139), following Rv 3:19; C 602.61–603.70 (L 2:249): *"Solent pii patres bonique magistri, postquam in disciplina filiorum correctioneque discipulorum virgam cedentem consumpserint, virgam ipsam ignem mittere: idem proculdubio faciet ille Pater noster, qui est in celis* (Mt 6:9), *de malignis spiritibus atque impiis hominibus, qui sunt baculus et virga eius in illorum flagellatione, quos his arguit et castigat* (Rv 3:19) *super suis erroribus, ut ad suam tandem hereditatem probati ac digni perveniant."* B 2:51.138–52.150, 2:53.176–94 (L 1:134–35), following Ps 26:2–3, 2 Cor 12:7–9, Heb 12:6–8.

3. B 2:15.386 (L 1:116): *". . . per magistre aduersitatis eruditionem in se reuertitur; . . ."*; B 2:17.447–54 (L 1:117), especially 447: *". . . ad seram penitentiam interius aspirando reuocat"*; B 2:18.473–81 (L 1:117).

of being corrected will purge the sins admitted in the first step. But the prodigal son will now have hope of a heavenly reward because, as a faithful son of God, he would have fled those situations and behaviors that are neither related to nor enkindled by the love of God. This admission of guilt and willingness to work hard to make amends leads the prodigal son to the third step: a sincere, inner change that opens his heart to God's aid. Following Ambrose, Clamanges taught simply: *". . . venit ad penitentiam sed nundum peruenit ad gratie perfectionem."* The result would be an inner conversion achieved when the prodigal son's bad deeds, tears, and mourning are restored to light by God's mercy and by the son's own purgation through adversity. This process leads to his humble request for heavenly aid. The assurance of the son's reconciliation with God is the ring and banquet the father gives him. Clamanges employed Ambrose and Bede's commentary on this parable in describing the ring as the sign of faith by which the soul is pledged to God. The son's faults are covered because he is truly reformed by his penitent action, which is why the ring is rightly placed on his hand since faith without works is dead. The banquet is the fruit of his penitence. The prodigal son moves from death to life, from being lost to found because his active penitence and perseverance through adversity produce his sincere, inner conversion.[4]

Clamanges frequently illustrated the important role of adversity in personal reform with the scriptural imagery of purgative fire. Using his favored image of impending destruction to signal a time for penitence, for example, Clamanges concluded *De ruina et reparacione Ecclesie* with a warning that his readers should remember the fiery fate of Sodom and Gomorrah, which had failed to repent. Elsewhere, he turned to Isaiah to make his case on a more individual level: the prophet was purified when

4. B 2:19.496–20.531 (L 1:118), following Rom 10:10, Ps 38:118, and Ambrose, PL 16:1044: *"Praecedit poenitentia, sequitur gratia."* B 2:23.605–16 (L 1:120), following Ps 59:11, Tb 2:6; B 2:24.636–40 (L 1:121): *"Annulus arra vel signaculum fidei est, in qua anima fidelis a Deo desponsatur, quod per culpam obnubilatur aut deletur, per penitentiam vero in integrum reformatur. Qui recte in manu datur, vt quod corde creditur aut ore promitur opere perficiatur, quoniam fides sine operibus mortua est,"* following Ambrose, PL 15:1761, and Bede, PL 92:525. B 2:25.654–55 (L 1:121): *"Epulari vero cum patre est post dignos penitentie fructus peractos. . . ."* Bérier noted the importance of the prodigal son's personal conversion in Clamanges' sermon: B 1:xii–xiii.

an angel touched his lips with fire from God's altar. Such an example of correction and purification is important for Clamanges because fire not only purifies the heart but burns away sin. In the central treatise for this aspect of his thought, *De prosperitate aduersitatis,* Clamanges wrote that purgation by fire and tribulation toughens the mind, strengthens the body, and illuminates. He continued with this imagery throughout *De prosperitate aduersitatis:* Christians will be tested, strengthened, and purified by God through fire just as a clay pot is hardened by the flame.[5] The example of metals tested in a fire that burns away their impurities also illustrates Clamanges' constant theme: God repairs His children by destruction and tests them by tribulation.[6]

Tapping into the Christocentric focus of late medieval spirituality, Clamanges supported his imagery of God repairing through destruction by focusing on Jesus' example. The dominant citation from the New Testament was the gospels' description of Christ cleansing the temple of the moneychangers. He had used this image in letters to Gerson and Benedict XIII in 1398 to spur them to take action to restore unity to the Church. Clamanges returned to the gospel accounts of Christ cleansing the temple three times in his 1412 treatise sent to Gerson, *Contra prelatos symoniacos,* when discussing how to rid the Church of simony. Perhaps most strikingly, in *De ruina* Clamanges brought together the image of purifying fire with the state of the late medieval Church and the need for Christ's corrective hand. There he addressed Christ directly, asking him

5. Coville, *Le Traité,* 156, following Gn 19:23–25; B 2:115.321–23, 328–31 (d'Achery 1:475). Clamanges made this dual point with reference to Isaiah and the burning coal of the seraph that touched his lips at B 2:116.350–53 (d'Achery 1:476): *"Denique ad Ysaiam missus ait Seraphim: Ecce tetigi hoc labia tua et auferetur iniquitas tua, et peccatum tuum mundabitur* (Is 6:7). *Certum est autem non labiorum tactu sed cordis, peccata mundari."* See also B 2:59.355–58 (L 1:138), 2:61.394–99 (L 1:139), following Sir 27:5.

6. Among many examples, see *De prosperitate aduersitatis* at B 2:59.342–44 (L 1:138): *"Non ibi aurum recipietur quod non hic in fornace probatum tribulationis ab omni sorde et labe purum erit."* See also B 2:60.382–89 (L 1:139): *"Deus nempe ad nos per tribulationen non verbo sed verbere loquitur. Corda autem que per hunc ignem non emolliuntur terrena nimis et lutea sunt: terram enim solet et lutum ignis indurare, qui dura etiam cogit metalla liquescere, a quibus ea purificando scoriam excoquit* (Is 1:25), *rubiginem aufert* (Prv 25:4), *sordes omnes educit; vnde de Domino per Malachiam scribitur: Sedebit conflans et emundans argentum, et purgabit filios Leui* (Mal 3:3)." In a letter written in 1395, relatively early in his career, Clamanges also noted many errors needed correction, just as tools must be sharpened or polished: C 19:163–66 (L 2:13).

to purge and repair His Church by fire just as gold and silver are purified in a furnace.[7] Clamanges turned to past examples of Christ's correction: He directed Christians to live rightly by allowing persecutions. These trials steered Christians away from the love of worldly things, cleansed their impurities, and helped them to reform while preparing for their eternal reward. Those who had been reformed would then enjoy eternal salvation, while those who had failed to reform would descend into hell. In *Contra prelatos symoniacos,* Clamanges repeated that Christians who had pursued worldliness would ultimately be separated from those who had lived according to the spirit. He concluded ominously with John the Baptist's prophecy: Jesus was coming to divide the wheat from the chaff with His winnowing fan.[8]

Clamanges did not hold, however, that physical and spiritual purgation would necessarily result in a successful transformation of the Christian experiencing adversity. Not everyone who was tried would be able to stand up to the test, to achieve personal reform, and therefore to reach salvation. In *De prosperitate aduersitatis,* he cited Jeremiah to conclude a lengthy discussion of purgation by fire. Clamanges warned that just as every metal is not strengthened in the furnace, not every Christian tested would be purged and found worthy of the heavenly reward. In such a situation, the fires would burn in vain and the sins of these unworthy Christians would not be consumed. The Lord will reject Christians who did not truly purge their hearts just as impure silver, which does not pass the test of fire, is cast aside. Clamanges' discussions of the experience of adversity thus took on a prophetic tone of warning, as did his poem on the Schism, *Deploratio calamitatis ecclesiastice,* where Clamanges predicted God would send destruction and the river Styx would flow over the world. Peace and pacts of friendship would be destroyed; all sorts of war, tumult, and plagues would be unleashed. In a letter to Gerson, Clamanges had also issued a warning: unless learned doctors and ecclesiastics set themselves against the trickery rampant within the Church, it

7. C 65.83–96 (L 2:41–42), 90.289–92 (L 2:55); B 2:139.100–11 (L 1:162), 2:141.158–59 (L 1:162–63), 2:148.344–47 (L 1:166); Coville, *Le Traité,* 154–55.

8. C 177.83–178.111 (L 2:105–6); B 2:148.341–42 (L 1:166), following Jer 15:7, Mt 3:12, Lk 3:17.

would be necessary to destroy the entire system that gave rise to these problems.[9]

Clamanges recognized the *reformatio personalis* was a difficult path upon which to embark, yet he still stressed it was a spiritual journey worth pursuing because the experience of adversity could lead to salvation. This conception of the *via purgativa,* growing from the Pauline core of 2 Cor 12:9 that virtue is perfected in infirmity, was described fully in *De prosperitate aduersitatis,* written in the context of Clamanges' own difficult personal experiences at the start of his second active exile. The theme also appears in numerous letters and other treatises, but particularly in *De prosperitate aduersitatis* Clamanges persuasively made his case that without taking the first, essential step of embracing adversity in order to achieve personal reform, all other efforts at late medieval reform were doomed. Specifically, Clamanges sought to help individual Christians pursue the fruits of trial, especially in light of the invitation to imitate the life and sufferings of Christ. Clamanges also wanted his readers to appreciate a paradox: while adversity leads to heaven, prosperity is the devil's trick and leads only to hell. He used examples from the Old Testament and drew on his own experiences with adversity to illustrate these points. Finally, he exhorted his readers to recognize and fight the battle between spirit and body at the core of the struggle for personal reform.

Clamanges' initial point in *De prosperitate aduersitatis* was that learning to appreciate and live by the virtues, which are some of the first fruits of bearing adversity, leads to further happiness. Far from being broken, the Christian surviving adversity by leaning on the virtues will eventually bear obstacles with a peaceful and tranquil spirit, even with a sense of humor. He will soon cultivate a desire to embrace more adversity, following the example of the Fathers and others who happily and fervently sought to attain their heavenly reward. Similarly, in an undated letter written from Paris to a new Celestine monk, Clamanges advised his correspondent to follow those who had been most tested and to learn the lessons given in their examples of bearing adversity. Although in this

---

9. B 2:60.389–61.393 (L 1:139), following Jer 6:29–30; C 645:9–15, 20–26 (Coville, *Recherches,* 261.6–13, 17–23), following Mt 24:6–7, Mk 13:7–8, Lk 21:9–11; C 64.69–65.73 (L 2:41).

treatise and letter Clamanges spoke only generally about the virtues and the lessons of others' examples, in *De fructu heremi,* written during the same period as *De prosperitate aduersitatis,* he delineated them by equating the virtues with the gifts of the Holy Spirit, including joy, patience, goodness, and faith.[10] But he also emphasized that a Christian's life would always be balanced between good and bad times, as he wrote to his friend Gérard Machet in 1412. Both the sweet times and the bitter trials would teach and heal the Christian. Consequently, the Christian should learn to live with adversity, just as Christ had accepted the bitter cup of His passion in Gethsemane and the sons of Judah had learned to live with their enemies the Jebusites when they failed to drive them from Jerusalem. Clamanges concluded this letter to Machet with an encouraging promise of an ultimate gain. Among the joys and prayers of human life would be mixed errors, anxieties, and other troubles. This combination of experiences would produce both gain and decay. Once the bad had been endured, however, the faithful, diligent Christian would reach a perfect state of unwavering goodness that would fully satisfy all desires.[11]

Clamanges described another fruit of bearing adversity: a shared spiritual journey. The suffering man does not undergo trial alone but shares his sorrow and pain with others. Persecuted Christians must bear their common tribulations together, sustaining each other through pain and purgation. Not only is the Christian joined in his suffering with his fellows, but the Lord is with all of them in their struggle. On this point Clamanges quoted the Psalmist: "I am with him in tribulation. . . . I will deliver him and glorify him." He buttressed his argument with Jesus' statement "What you did for the least of my brothers, you did for me," and Jesus' question to Saul: "Why do you persecute me?"[12]

10. B 2:47.22–25, 47.27–48.32, 48.36–41 (L 1:132–33); C 188.99–104 (L 2:112); B 2:32.169–71 (L 1:124).

11. Dario Cecchetti, "Nicolas de Clamanges e Gérard Machet. Contributo allo studio dell'epistolario di Nicolas de Clamanges," *Atti dell'Academia delle scienze di Torino* 100 (1965–66): 189.32–190.41, 190.50–56, following Mt 26:39, Mk 14:36, Lk 22:42, Jos 15:63, Jgs 1:21. See also Pierre Santoni, "Les lettres de Nicolas de Clamanges à Gérard Machet. Un humaniste devant la crise du royaume et de l'Église (1410–1417)," *Mélanges de l'École française de Rome. Moyen Âge temps modernes* 99 (1987): 808.

12. B 2:48.47–51 (L 1:133); B 2:49.57–58 (L 1:133), following Mt 25:40; B 2:49.60–61 (L 1:133), following Acts 9:4, 22:7, 26:14; B 2:49.67–69 (L 1:133), following Ps 91:15.

This image of God's companionship and support during a time of persecution was taken much further by Clamanges as he continued to elaborate the fruits of adversity. In *De prosperitate aduersitatis* and *De fructu heremi*, Clamanges demonstrated some of his most impassioned and rhetorical writing when presenting purgative Christian suffering as a way of imitating the life of Christ, a common late medieval focus of devotional piety that he married with his foundational principle of *reformatio personalis*. The fact that the suffering Christian actually imitates Christ leads Clamanges to ask his reader what greater glory there can be than to walk in His footsteps. He emphasized in *De prosperitate aduersitatis* that Christ's whole life, all Jesus had done and said, was meant to teach. Jesus Himself mandated the Christian should follow His example: He explicitly told His disciples they should serve each other as He had done by washing their feet at the last supper. Clamanges stressed that the most powerful example is Jesus' death on the cross, by which He taught Christians to bear hardship with patience and to understand their suffering within a broader context. Following Christ, Clamanges continued, Christians must take up their own crosses. Here again the *imitatio Christi* was expressly invoked by Clamanges, this time in the words of Paul, who exhorted the Christians at Corinth to "Be imitators of me, as I am of Christ." Clamanges seemed to soften this mandate, however, by pointing out that Jesus' death on His own cross enabled His followers to serve with easier burdens. Thus, Jesus calls Christians not to heavy burdens, but away from work and toward rest. Again, Clamanges offered a rhetorical challenge: Who would not respond to such a call to follow Christ?[13]

Interwoven with Clamanges' discussion of imitating Christ is the imagery of Christians as soldiers. If soldiers carry a king's arms and insignia for worldly glory, Clamanges wrote in *De prosperitate aduersitatis,* then true soldiers of Christ ought not to shun the Christian insignia

13. B 2:49.77–50.90 (L 1:133), following 1 Jn 2:6, Jn 13:15, Mt 16:24, Lk 9:23; B 2:50.96–97 (L 1:134), following 1 Cor 11:1; B 2:51.121–35 (L 1:134), following Mt 11:28–30. Although Clamanges did not explicitly cite other similar messages in the Pauline epistles, possible influences may have been Phil 3:17 (a citation Clamanges used elsewhere) where Paul encouraged his listeners to imitate him and others by following their model, and Eph 5:1–2 where he urged the Ephesians to imitate God and live in love as Christ lived and gave His life for God's children.

or arms—that is, Christ's cross—but embrace it in imitation of Paul, that strongest Christian soldier who gloried in Christ's cross. Clamanges reminded his readers that taking up Christ's cross and fighting for one's soul entails persecution. But, he promised in *De fructu heremi,* whoever exalts in Christ's cross will have his sins forgiven. He used martial imagery to contrast worldly with heavenly glory when describing the soldier who leaves his home and family to expose himself to danger in order to protect his friends and thereby win temporal honor. He deprives himself of luxuries, fears no trouble, and avoids no danger; he goes to his death expecting no mercy other than vain honor or the fleeting glory of the world. This being the case, Clamanges concluded, what ought we to expect from the analogous Christian soldier who seeks not a brief but an eternal glory? Moreover, if a king exposes himself to death for his reputation and to ransom his least servant, what labors, dangers, or burdens ought he to undergo for the sake of his soul? Clamanges drew on Tertullian's language calling Christians to an eternal prize earned through service in God's army. Christian soldiers, Tertullian explained, go to battle after training like an athlete in harsh and austere conditions that toughened body and spirit.[14]

Clamanges portrayed adversity, not prosperity, as spiritually efficacious, desirable, and purgative. While prosperity appeared to lead to benefits, these were worldly and fleeting; prosperity was trickery used by the devil to lead people to hell. Adversity appears as something to be avoided in this life, but it actually leads to eternal life and should be pursued by Christians. He contrasted corrective adversity with subversive prosperity, asking the Christian to be mindful of the essential difference: "Indeed it is the bitter sting of scourges by which we are corrected by God, but we are separated from God by the sting of the worst sins, which more freely creep up in peace and prosperity."[15] Like a fisherman

14. B 2:50.90–96 (L 1:133–34), following Gal 6:14; B 2:66.531–32 (L 1:141), following 2 Tm 3:12; B 2:42.451–53 (L 1:130); B 2:50.98–51.118 (L 1:134). Cecchetti identified the Tertullian influence, found at CSEL 76:4, 4–5 [*Ad martyras,* 3].

15. B 2:62.443–45 (L 1:140): *"Amara quippe est amaritudo flagellorum quibus a Deo corripimur, sed amaritudo amarissima peccatorum quibus a Deo separamur, que in pace ac prosperitate licentius obrepunt."* Clamanges later in this treatise cited Paul's use of Moses as an example of someone choosing adversity with God over temporal prosperity: B 2:65.516–18 (L 1:141), following Heb 11:24–25.

using bait and hook, the devil deceives with prosperity and temporal happiness, which lead only to falsehood and trouble. The unsuspecting Christian is hooked like a fish by his own desires and brings upon himself his own woes. In *De prosperitate aduersitatis,* Clamanges quoted Solomon as a witness to bolster his point that the prosperity of fools destroys them. While adversity leads to the understanding and practice of the virtues, prosperity conversely leads to the vices: luxury, arrogance, greed, envy, neglect, drunkenness, anger, and impatience, all of which emasculate men, sap the vigor of their spirits, and stir up their desires. In turn, the allure of worldly prosperity results in troubled minds and tired bodies. Anything that people consider to be desirable in prosperity, Clamanges summarized, actually produces only sorrow, bitterness, fear, danger, and ultimately ruin.[16]

Adversity, on the other hand, yields rich fruits for pious sons of God who are spiritually strengthened by labors, scourges, poverty, and persecution. They hope for eternity, are careful to avoid worldly consolation, and are cautious about the dangers surrounding them. Fleeing from worldly consolations, they resist delight in pomp, glory, luxury, and ambition. Clamanges followed patristic models that tied physical to spiritual health. For Clamanges, adversity is like restorative medicine by which God calls the Christian back to health from the immoderate excesses of prosperity and redirects him to a proper disposition. The human heart, restless and suffering infirmity, ought to turn to God for its medicine as did Hezekiah, king of Judah. All worldly and carnal desires that do not promote physical and spiritual health must be avoided; doctors and antidotes should be sought.[17]

Clamanges offered historical and personal models to complement his scriptural examples; these illustrated his contention that adversity leads to physical health and spiritual triumph. He tried to prove that the Church, though currently beset by a myriad of problems, had suffered

16. B 2:54.220–55.230 (L 1:136); B 2:66.533 (L 1:142), following Prv 1:32; B 2:56.278–57.282 (L 1:137); B 2:62.446–63.463 (L 1:140).

17. B 2:55.236–47 (L 1:136); B 2:56.257–68, 271–76 (L 1:136–37); B 2:57.283–86 (L 1:137); B 2:62.436–42 (L 1:140), following Is 38:16. Many of the Fathers referred to God the Father or Christ as a great or divine physician: Rudolph Arbesmann, "The Concept of *Christus medicus* in St. Augustine," *Traditio* 10 (1954): 5–7, 27–28.

and survived before, even emerging stronger because of the tribulation. Clamanges in this way linked past lessons of purgative suffering with his norm of the utility of adversity to offer hope for the present lamentable situations.

Throughout the world, he wrote, the Church is under attack: she is torn apart by vice, ambition, and dereliction of good works and spiritual duties. Many Christians live by the vices: far from the life of virtues, they lapse into luxury and leisure. Yet during a similar time of trouble, namely the persecution of the martyrs, the Church grew stronger. Earlier, the more the Hebrews suffered while in captivity in Egypt, the more they prospered and even multiplied. Turning to a secular example, Clamanges noted that the struggles of the Punic Wars had strengthened Rome. Here Clamanges extended his comparison of the utility of adversity and the danger of prosperity: once Carthage had been defeated, Rome devolved into laziness and vice—an enemy from within worse than the outside threat of Carthage. Without the adversity that strengthened her, Rome drowned in her own prosperity. Clamanges added that the same problem beset the Israelites once they established themselves in Canaan after many difficult battles under Joshua's leadership.[18]

Ultimately, physical and spiritual adversity will lead the faithful, persevering Christian to heaven, Clamanges summarized in a key passage in *De prosperitate aduersitatis.* Only by means of trials will the Christian enter the kingdom of heaven through the narrow gate. Despite this fact, Clamanges observed, many in his contemporary world were on their way to hell because they followed the alluring path of prosperity even though the choice seemed clear: to live forever with Abraham in heaven like the poor man Lazarus or to burn eternally in Gehenna like the rich man who had denied Lazarus food. Faced with this choice, and having been told earthly trials yield heavenly rewards, would not anyone choose passing poverty and infirmity over eternal damnation, Clamanges again asked rhetorically. He expressed amazement that so few people worked toward their own salvation and that, while some acted to subdue their

---

18. B 2:61.400–403 (L 1:139), following Ex 1:7–12; B 2:61.416–62.421 (L 1:139); B 2:62.425–36 (L 1:139–40). Tertullian and Augustine noted Christ as healer allowed martyrdom and other sufferings to occur in order to bring Christians to salvation: Arbesmann, "The Concept of *Christus medicus*," 6, 21–23.

desires through penance, others did so only superficially or falsely. They may say they fear hell, but they defraud, lie, rape, and are lax: their actions betray their words. Clamanges warned, however, that they will be known by their deeds and not their words.[19]

Clamanges' emphasis on personal purgation also grew from his own experiences, which he used to demonstrate first-hand lessons of the *via purgativa*. In several letters he offered consolation to d'Ailly and Gerson, as the three of them lived through their exiles brought on by the French subtraction of obedience from Benedict XIII. In August 1398, Clamanges wrote to Gerson from Langres, where he was recuperating from a very serious case of plague which, he told his friend, had carried him *ad portas usque mortis*. Clamanges said the experience left him grateful and renewed his commitment to serve God and to follow the proper path to salvation. By bearing hardship and the turmoil of their era, their circle of friends would be corrected and learn to appreciate the Lord's saving power and peace, just as Peter and the other disciples were saved when Jesus calmed the stormy seas. Similarly, Clamanges told d'Ailly in 1402 that only through the current trials could God reform the Church. It was necessary for God to chastise their sins and to purge their arrogance, greed, simony, and ambition. In this way, the core vices would be rooted out and Christ's spouse, the deformed Church, would be returned to the pristine state and proper ways of her youth. Clamanges therefore applied the lessons of adversity to his own life as well as to the Church at large. He was willing, at least in this case, to preach what he had practiced.[20]

Clamanges threw down a practical spiritual challenge, exhorting his readers to make the choice for heaven and to demonstrate their decision by faithful actions instead of meaningless words. The Christian must strive for heaven over hell by condemning and spurning secular luxuries (prosperity) while persevering and bearing suffering (adversity). Though man's life is drudgery according to Job, Clamanges countered with Paul's

19. B 2:57.294–58.313, 2:58.316–19 (L 1:137–38), following Lk 13:24, 16:19–31.

20. C 97.10–98.13 (L 2:59); C 98.21–29, 34–37 (L 2:60), following Mt 8:23–27, Mk 4:36–40, Lk 8:22–25; C 177.63–70 (L 2:105). André Combes surveyed the d'Ailly-Clamanges correspondence from this period, but he did not place the letters within the context of Clamanges' reform thought: "Sur les 'lettres de consolation' de Nicolas de Clamanges à Pierre d'Ailly," *Archives d'histoire doctrinale et littéraire du Moyen Âge* 13 (1940–42): 359–89.

counsel to Timothy that the athlete competing earnestly will earn his crown of victory. Finding the same promise of heaven echoed in the letter of James, Clamanges noted that the man who suffers temptation and trial will receive the crown of life.[21] This conscious choice between heaven and hell represented for Clamanges an important turning point in the spiritual journey toward personal reform: the moment when a Christian realizes the path back to God and salvation lies within his suffering and adversity. In this way, the fruits of greed—the burdens which Clamanges said would be the products of worldly prosperity—would ironically be for some people their first step toward reconciliation with God. The repentant Christian in this scenario would be like the returning prodigal son embraced by his father. Reaching again for vegetative imagery, Clamanges illustrated this point by describing how sweetness may be found among bitterness: thorns guard flowers, honey collects between thickets of bees, corn grows among weeds, manured vines lead to wine. He then linked these examples to the purgative suffering at the heart of the active *reformatio personalis*. Christians are analogously cultivated, attaining virtue and bearing good fruit by continuous spiritual labor.[22]

To recapitulate the centrality of purgative personal reform in Clamanges' thought, we turn to a letter in which he described the battle between body and spirit that traps the individual Christian between Christ and the devil. This letter, which draws heavily on Pauline imagery to gather together many of Clamanges' points concerning the *via purgativa* and the utility of adversity, was written to Gerson sometime after 1408 from Clamanges' retreat at Fontaine-au-Bois. He returned to the theme of 2 Cor 12:9: "Virtue is perfected in infirmity." Infirmity, he wrote to Gerson, is to be valued as greater than good health. But, he added paradoxically, a corrupted body may also handicap the spirit by distracting it from its purpose. Thus, the body and the spirit fight each other, as Paul told the Galatians. Though inspired by heaven, the Christian is at the same time strapped down by his own body. Pulled by body

21. B 2:58.325–28 (L 1:138); B 2:58.333–59.339 (L 1:138), following Jb 7:1, 2 Tm 2:5; B 2:59.344–45 (L 1:138), following Jas 1:12.

22. B 2:64.479–65.502 (L 1:140–41), following Heb 12:11, Gn 3:18; B 2:65.528–66.529 (L 1:141), following Lk 15:11–32.

and spirit, the Christian is weakened and caught in the middle.[23] Having laid down the seeming contradiction, Clamanges drove home his message to Gerson: the suffering Christian is spiritually strengthened by the fruits of adversity within this very struggle between body and spirit. The suffering Christian imitates Christ at the same time he follows the example of Paul's imitation of Christ. But while Paul lamented the restraints of his sinful body, Clamanges recognized that the way of perfection is contained within the very trials of trying to break free of such restraints. Why else, he asked Gerson, would anyone seek to follow the example of Christ? Once again employing the example of the soldier to illustrate his point, Clamanges noted the reward for the Christian would be like the sweetness the soldier experiences after he has borne his labors and has overcome his personal desires. Clamanges concluded this letter to Gerson by encouraging him to bear his trials like Paul and the saints. He comforted Gerson by noting Paul became deeply discouraged because of the persecution he and his companions experienced, suffering that seemed to them so beyond their ability to endure they even despaired of living. But bearing the body's hardships, Clamanges promised Gerson, leads to the death of vice in a Christian and then to a spiritual life of virtue.[24]

SPIRITUAL TOOLS

Clamanges took pains to convince his readers of the utility of adversity, but he also tried to persuade them they had to do more than simply appreciate the fruits of suffering. They had to actively embrace purgation for their personal correction and salvation. For Clamanges, this action entailed the humble, fearful acceptance of God's rectifying chastisement. These elements of fear and humility reflected scriptural, patristic, and

---

23. C 286.14–18, 20–22 (L 2:177); C 287.28–29 (L 2:177); C 288.63–65 (L 2:178); C 288.89–289.99 (L 2:178), following Gal 5:17 (see also Rom 7:14–23). In *De prosperitate aduersitatis,* Clamanges also stressed divine aid versus the devil in this battle: B 2:67.562–72 (L 1:142).

24. C 287.34–39 (L 2:177); C 289.109–290.140 (L 2:178–79), following Rom 7:24, 1 Cor 4:16, 1 Cor 11:1, Phil 3:17, 1 Thes 1:6, 2 Cor 1:8. Clamanges also made this point in *De prosperitate aduersitatis,* B 2:66.539–41 (L 1:142): *"Cum enim inter animam et corpus, inter carnem et spiritum semper bellum sit, quanto caro viribus inferior tanto est spiritus ipse robustior. . . ."*

late medieval influences. In the Old Testament, the word "fear" connotes a reverence for God that culminates in adoration while often entailing a feeling of dread directed toward impending divine chastisement. Within the Hebrews' relationship with God, this type of fear of God represented religious piety; acting on this fearful piety, the Hebrews pleased God by fulfilling His moral commands. In the New Testament, fear was more often depicted as a virtue that led to salvation. For Augustine, humility was the key to perfection, a model of which was offered by Christ in His incarnation. In his *De doctrina Christiana*, Augustine noted as well that fear and piety grounded in humility led to knowledge of God. In the sixth-century *Regula* of Benedict, fearing God is the first of the twelve degrees of humility and leads to eternal life. This biblical and patristic understanding of fear and humility entered the mainstream of medieval spirituality and was especially evident in the late medieval tradition. Christ was particularly offered as an example of humility and obedience in the writings of the leaders of the *devotio moderna,* near contemporaries of Clamanges.[25]

Clamanges' position that fear and humility were important tools for spiritual growth is concisely presented in the exhortation he sent to the young Celestine. Fear and humility should be the new monk's rocks and spiritual foundation. Persevering with these tools, his spiritual progress in virtue would increase; without them, his spiritual life would topple. Quoting Jesus, Clamanges continued this imagery: a house built on rock would survive rain, floods, and wind, while the house built on sand would topple. Humility is a root in the ground that will deflect the Christian from a dangerous spiritual trap: the desire to walk according

---

25. *Dictionary of Biblical Theology,* 2d ed., 174–75, s.v. "fear of God"; *Dictionnaire de la Bible,* 2:1100, s.v. "crainte de Dieu," by F. Vigouroux; for a fuller treatment, see B. Olivier, *La crainte de Dieu comme valeur religieuse dans l'Ancien Testament* (Paris: Office Général du Livre, 1960). Arbesmann noted Augustine linked his image of Christ as physician with the example of His humility in order to counter the human sin of pride: "The Concept of *Christus medicus,*" 8–17, especially 10 nn. 69–72. See also Augustine, *On Christian Doctrine,* trans. D. W. Robertson, Jr. (New York: Macmillan/Library of Liberal Arts, 1958), 38–39 [Bk. 2, ch. 7, pts. 9–10]. For Benedict's treatment of humility, see Owen Chadwick, trans., *Western Asceticism* (Philadelphia: Westminster Press, 1958), 301–304 [Ch. 7]. On the *devotio moderna,* see Otto Gründler, "*Devotio Moderna,*" in *Christian Spirituality: High Middle Ages and Reformation,* ed. Jill Raitt (New York: Crossroad, 1988), 182–84, 189–91.

to the greatness of the world. Fear helps the Christian remain strong and reminds him he cannot live apart from God's perfecting mandates nor by his own deeds, which offend God; rather, God gives the aid that the Christian seeks. He again turned to vegetative imagery to illustrate how fear and humility aid the young tree by helping it to grow, bear fruit, and survive troubles, just as a tree planted near running water yields fruit in its proper season. The monk should strive to remain unshaken, unlike a new stalk that bends with the wind. Playing on the word "Celestine," the religious order that his correspondent had just joined, Clamanges wrote that the monk had been planted in heavenly soil. With such roots planted firmly in his heart, he could reach the heights of heaven and produce the greatest yield. Moreover, the monk—the young tree—had been planted by God the farmer of heaven *(celestis te plantari voluit agricola).* Tended by God, he would grow in faith.[26]

But elsewhere in his correspondence where Clamanges treated fear, there was a decreased emphasis on nurturing and a greater stress on the jeopardy into which many Christians without fear placed themselves. Clamanges told Nicolas de Baye that fear turns Christians away from worldly ambition and glory; without fear, they may stray from what is right because of ignorance. He expressed to Gerson his desire for Christians to turn back to God from worldliness in fear. Without this fear of God, fools provoke their own trouble, thinking there is no God. Clamanges concluded another letter to de Baye by stating flatly no vices or passions could be conquered, indeed no justice could be accomplished, without the fear of God.[27]

Clamanges was also aware the Christian on the journey to contemplate God in humility and fear needed to be in the proper setting to do so. *Reformatio personalis* required solitude and silence. In *De fructu here-*

---

26. C 186.20–187.67 (L 2:111), following Mt 7:24–27, Lk 6:48–49, Ps 1:3, Jer 17:8, Phil 3:20; C 188.72–74, 77–83 (L 2:111–12), following 1 Cor 3:6. In *De prosperitate aduersitatis,* Clamanges described the grace of humility as the guardian and root of all virtue; arrogance leads to sins and vices: B 2:54.205–207 (L 1:136).

27. C 466.165–72 (L 2:278), following Rom 11:20; C 282.33–56 (L 2:174–75); C 285.136–51 (L 2:176), following Ps 14:1; C 472.182–87 (L 2:282). On the relationship between Clamanges and de Baye, see Alfred Coville, *Gontier et Pierre Col et l'humanisme en France au temps de Charles VI* (Paris: Droz, 1934), 92–94.

mi, Clamanges again urged his readers to imitate Christ: Jesus taught more about triumphing over the enemy in His solitude and silence than while in the busy world. As he described adversity in *De filio prodigo* as a *magister,* here he presented solitude as a master who required daily exercise to instruct.[28] Once more Clamanges built on personal experience to comment on the need for quiet and solitude in order for the individual Christian to reform himself before he proceeded to broader institutional goals. Clamanges searched for a calm port for himself, finding it first in 1398 at Langres where he declared he could be more productive, useful, and prayerful. By contrast, Paris and Avignon were full of pitfalls that pulled him away from quiet thought. Clamanges considered Paris too hectic, offering interruptions to work and enticements against living a moral life, as is clear from letters he wrote to his Parisian friends, notably Jean de Montreuil and Gérard Machet. Paris was so dangerous, Clamanges declared vividly to Montreuil in December 1398 from Langres, mothers should cry when their sons begin to study there in the same way they lament their sons going off to war. Earlier that year, in the summer, he had told Montreuil from Châlons-sur-Marne that Paris was a labyrinth of courts and princely service that should be avoided. It would be, he warned, very difficult to escape from Paris.[29]

Clamanges' deep loathing of Paris is best explored in a long letter written to Machet from Fontaine-au-Bois ca. 1411–14. Taking as his starting point Is 48:20 ("Babylon is to be fled"), Clamanges offered his friend an invective against Paris, which he equated with Babylon. He cited a series of biblical accounts of the faithful abandoning dangerous places. Abraham emigrated from the region of his birth because of idol worship there; Noah built the ark to save his family from the flood that destroyed

28. B 2:29.89–92, 2:29.107–30.108 (L 1:123). For evidence of Petrarch's influence on Clamanges concerning the solitary life, see Cecchetti, *Petrarca, Pietramala e Clamanges. Storia di una "querelle" inventata* (Paris: Éditions CEMI, 1982), 63–89.

29. C 93.5–9 (L 2:57); C 133.27–30 (L 2:79). François Bérier noted Clamanges' personal preference for solitude in "La figure du clerc dans le *'De studio theologico'* de Nicolas de Clamanges," *Travaux de linguistique et de littérature* 21 (1983): 95–96. On the relationship between Clamanges and Montreuil, see Ornato, *Jean Muret,* passim, and Coville, *Gontier et Pierre Col,* 72–98. On Clamanges and Machet, see Cecchetti, "Nicolas de Clamanges e Gérard Machet," and Santoni, "Les lettres de Nicolas de Clamanges à Gérard Machet."

the evil people around them; Lot left Sodom and Gomorrah; Moses led the Hebrews out of Egypt because of their enslavement and the fact they could not sacrifice to their God; Joseph took Mary and the baby Jesus to safety in Egypt; even Christ told his disciples to leave a place where they were not welcomed. Following these Old and New Testament examples, Clamanges concluded the Christian must physically escape from a place where he cannot live according to God and where evil surrounds the Christian because vices run rampant and unchecked. Paris is just such a trap for Christians: there it is easier for the good to fall into the bad ways that surround them than it is for the bad to turn to correct paths. Clamanges again employed rhetorical questions to make his point. How could a sane person not fear living where all are insane? he asked Machet. Who could live according to virtue in such a place and not fear being shipwrecked or burned by fire? Moreover, what should be fled more than immoral ways that go against divine laws and the good examples of the holy Fathers? The faithful Christian ought not to remain among such insanity where everything goes against God; where bad is called good; where evil actions challenge the ways of piety; where there is no remedy for these problems or help for salvation; and where no one fears divine retribution, everything is infected, and people compete for praise in their corruption. The Christian should leave such a place, shaking its dust from his feet.[30]

Apart from immorality, Clamanges saw city life as providing dangerous distractions and the near occasion of sin for the Christian seeking to reform his spiritual state. Though he did not name Paris in *De fructu heremi,* his statement that urban delights produce danger instead of fruit is clearly applicable to Paris. The problem, he wrote, is not so much the urban allures, but the failure of people to avoid them. The more troubling issue for Clamanges was not the outside distractions themselves—formidable though they were—but the inner distractions to the spirit they caused. As he wrote to Montreuil, city life simply presented too

---

30. C 454.15–456.61 (L 1:174–75); C 457.95–124 (L 1:175–76); C 458.145–459.167 (L 1:176–77), following Mt 10:23; C 459.171–460.213 (L 1:177), following Mt 10:14. Cecchetti dates the letter to sometime after 1411: C lxxii. Santoni posits it was written in late 1413 or early 1414: "Les lettres de Nicolas de Clamanges à Gérard Machet," 809–12.

much immorality, turmoil and, perhaps most significantly, too many distractions to prayerful thinking and studying.[31]

Clamanges' concern with inner turmoil is best illustrated, once more, by his letter to Machet on the theme "Babylon is to be fled." He warned his friend that the dangerous confusion of Babylon was actually within one's mind. A spiritual Babylon mirrored the physical Babylon. Inner peace must be sought and cannot be found when the spirit is a confused and distracted Babylon. The mind should be focused on the things of heaven, not on earthly matters. Against Machet, Clamanges noted it would be easier to find spiritual peace if one physically fled the infectious moral diseases of a crowded city. Machet contended that since the evils of Babylon were everywhere and for this reason could never physically be fled, following the command to flee Babylon meant spiritually avoiding evil wherever one was located. Clamanges held that in a place physically far from a distracting and immoral city one could more readily live in spiritual peace and sincere, pious devotion to God. The Christian would then be living in a world that was both physically and spiritually more Jerusalem than Babylon. In such a Jerusalem, he could withdraw into his own heart in solitude with only God for a companion. It would be much easier to settle into a quiet spirit and find happiness there than in the middle of a physical Babylon. This interpretation is supported by two letters from the same period in which Clamanges, following Augustine, contrasted the confusion of Babylon with Jerusalem, the vision of peace. Urging de Baye to find a quiet place and time to study Scripture diligently, Clamanges told him to flee Babylon and ascend Mt. Zion, the placid mount of contemplation where God lives. Elsewhere, he told Gontier Col that the turmoil of the French civil war brought to his mind the stark difference between service in peaceful Jerusalem and tumultuous Babylon.[32]

31. B 2:27.48–28.60 (L 1:122); C 134.65–66 (L 2:80): *". . . sed quod non tante hic occupationes tanteque turbinum inquietudines meum studium meamque quietem interpellent."* See also C 137.161–138.190 (L 2:82). Jerome also frequently stressed in his letters that living in a city presented distractions to perfection; he commended the peaceful life in the country to his correspondents. Jerome's ideals of absolute poverty and rural isolation, however, were mitigated over time: Steven D. Driver, "The Development of Jerome's Views on the Ascetic Life," *Recherches de théologie ancienne et médiévale* 62 (1995): 65–70.

32. C 460.214–25 (L 1:177), especially 214–17: *"Queris quon[i]am pergere possis, ubi non confusam invenias Babilonem, et sedem quietam nusquam [sic] vides, nisi in tranquilla pacate*

In *De filio prodigo,* Clamanges provided some nuance to these statements that Babylon must be fled physically. In this sermon, Clamanges noted the prodigal son was sent to a farm to mind the pigs. Clamanges interpreted the farm as Babylon, the dwelling place of demons. The task of minding the pigs represents man's carnal, worldly desires as the prodigal son participates in the sins of the flesh committed by Adam and Eve; he is thereby engrossed in evil and concupiscence. This description hints at the challenge to avoid Babylon spiritually while in the physical place of sin, akin to Machet's interpretation, although Clamanges had earlier in the sermon recommended the prodigal son's physical return from the region of sin and death to life, grace, and mercy in his father's house, where he would be one with God's spirit. Here Clamanges seemed to find an interpretation that included both his own and Machet's emphasis: while a physical journey is involved, the prodigal son comes to penitence not by his feet but in his heart, not by leaving a place but by changing his spirit.[33]

Clamanges' personal decision was to seek physically a quiet place, something he could not find in the Bablyon-like Paris and Avignon. It will be recalled Langres was the first of several retreats in Clamanges' career: there he spent his first active exile during the 1398–1403 French

---

mentis statione. Quasi non etiam illic sepe Babilon sit." C 461.252–462.263 (L 1:178): "*Si autem urbium habitationem ceteramque populi frequentiam, tanquam Babilonica contagione infectam, refugis, sunt loca ab urbibus secreta, pia Dei sinceritate servientium, sunt probate religiones, sunt devota monasteria, plus Iherusalem quam Babilonem redolentia, sunt denique, si omne humanum times consortium, loca solitaria, in quibus tecum habitare poteris et intra cor tuum secedere, tibi loqui tibi vivere, solum tue vite testem sociumque Deum habere, ubi illam postremo quietem animi, ad quam tantopere predicas fugiendum, multo liceat facilius moltoque felicius quam in media Babilone invenire.*" For the letters to de Baye and Col, see C 400.35–43 (L 2:237), following Ps 68:17 and Augustine's commentary on Ps 137:1 found in PL 37:1761; C 425.47–51 (L 2:260), citing Augustine's same comment again.

33. B 2:12.304–17 (L 1:114), following 1 Cor 6:17. B 2:13.332–40 (L 1:115): "*Que est hec villa diaboli in quam seruos suos ad porcorum pascionem mittit? Villa profecto ista Babilon est, que facta est habitatio demoniorum vt scribitur in Apocalipsi* (Jer 51:37, Rv 18:2). *Et quid per hanc villam nisi caro nostra, quid vero per porcos in ea pascendos nisi corporei sensus exprimuntur? Non quod illa aut isti a demone sint, vt perfidus Manicheus sentit, sed quod, ratione corruptionis ex peccato primi parentis in carne derelicte, ministerio carnis et sensuum qui a natura proni sunt ad malum, ad fedas concupiscentias hominibus immittendas velut oportunis instrumentis vtitur.*" B 2:20.529–30 (L 1:118): "*. . . venit non pede sed corde, nec locum relinquendo sed animum mutando. . . .*"

subtraction of obedience. He passed most of his second active exile in the Augustinian monastery at Fontaine-au-Bois with brief visits to Langres and the Carthusian monastery at Valprofonde. His appreciation of relative solitude and silence seems to have grown stronger during these two active exiles. After less than six months in Langres, Clamanges told Montreuil he was now able to refresh himself and turn his attention to reading, writing, and consideration of religious matters that had been pushed aside by the evils of the time. He was glad to be far from the turmoil of Paris and Avignon. In Langres, there were no distractions or allures of opulence and luxury; compared with Paris and Avignon, there was much frugality. The people worked hard and diligently with few signs of laziness. They were also devout and religious: seeking first the kingdom of God, they went to Mass before attending to their business. Clamanges told Montreuil, and his other friends by extension, that though he could not be physically with them in Paris he was still present to them through letters. He preferred Langres despite the fact that its cool air aggravated his rheumatism. Clamanges was happy there, asking his friends to stop trying to lure him back to Paris with the promise of offices and worldly glory that he claimed did not appeal to him.[34] He ended his December 1398 letter to Montreuil with a lyrical plea that his friends cease calling him back into the stormy seas of Paris from his peaceful retreat at Langres.[35]

Clamanges' appreciation of rural silence and solitude may have been offset by a certain careerism, however, indicating that in his own spiritu-

34. C 96.87–94 (L 2:58); C 132.3–133.18 (L 2:79); C 134.54–59 (L 2:80); C 135.116–137.155 (L 2:81); C 138.207–19 (L 2:82), following Mt 6:33; C 139.237–54, 260–64 (L 2:83). Although omitting Clamanges' reference to his rheumatism, Ornato debunked a previously held notion that Clamanges preferred Langres because of its better air: Ornato, *Jean Muret*, 66 n. 57. Clamanges' complaint that the dense air of Langres was unpleasant and the winters were harshly cold was repeated fourteen years later in a 1412 letter written to Machet during a brief return to Langres: Cecchetti, "Nicolas de Clamanges e Gérard Machet," 189.26–31. See also Santoni, "Les lettres de Nicolas de Clamanges à Gérard Machet," 807–808.

35. C 140.265–68 (L 2:83): "*Desiste igitur tandem, obsecro, ab hac tuta et pacata statione in mare me sevis fluotibus inquietum vocare tantaque instantia sollicitare, ut unde me vis turbinum expulit, illuc invalescente tempestate a portu recurram.*" Several months earlier, Clamanges had concluded another letter to Montreuil with the same plea: C 96.119–97.138 (L 2:59).

al journey he could fall prey to the very allures of Babylon against which he warned. Despite his ostensible protests that he enjoyed Langres, Clamanges left his canonry there and rejoined Benedict XIII's curia after France restored obedience to the Avignon papacy in May 1403. Then the trouble engendered in 1408 by charges that Clamanges had written Benedict's bull excommunicating Charles VI drove him once more from the Avignon papacy's curia and into his second active exile. Again experiencing quiet after tumult as he had in 1398, Clamanges in 1410 reiterated in *De fructu heremi* the lessons of silence and solitude he had begun to learn at Langres, as if realizing his return to the nexus of ecclesiastical politics had preempted his spiritual progress. Only in inner solitude could people be freed from the bonds of their tumultuous passions. Once the heart was emptied of these cares, it would be free to seek God and to meditate on divine matters. Meditation in turn would lead to inner purity, tranquility, and peace; these qualities are frequently assaulted because flattery and enticement distract the soul from Christ's help. Clamanges said he preferred a rustic life far from the worldly pleasures that offered nothing of spiritual permanence or profit.[36]

Clamanges stressed this ultimate goal of detached contemplation throughout his life. In one letter, he told Nicolas de Baye that only when earthly matters are spurned will the heart, alone and in silence, concern itself with meditation of heavenly matters. In another letter, he praised the abbot and monks at Soisson almost to the point of envy, noting that because they were free from secular affairs they could pray quietly with the Lord. Clamanges said he recognized that the tumult, ambition, and vices of the papal curia had worn him down. He preferred silent leisure, which allowed him to read and study without interruption. During his first active exile, Clamanges linked his experience with Jerome's: in their rural retreats they turned from the study of secular literature to Scripture, which they found more consoling. As he had done to Montreuil, Cla-

---

36. B 2:30.110–21 (L 1:123–24); B 2:37.319–23 (L 1:127). At length, Cecchetti treats Clamanges' preference for the country over the city as demonstrated by his poems: "'*Descriptio loci*' e '*Laudatio urbis.*' Persistenza e rinnovamento di strutture retoriche nell'opera di Nicolas de Clamanges," *Annali dell'Istituto Universitario Orientale* 35 (1993): 381–431. On Clamanges' praise of country living, see also Santoni, "Les lettres de Nicolas de Clamanges à Gérard Machet," 820–23.

manges asked de Baye why he continued to call him back to curial service, especially since Clamanges felt he could happily help the Church with his pen from his current silent spot without having to be in the curia, where he could not collect his thoughts or put them into words. He repeated his appreciation for the silence of his exiles in a letter written to the general council at Constance during some of its most turbulent deliberations: in his quiet exile he made greater spiritual progress in reading than in his whole time of study at Paris. He now happily enjoyed peace to write about the Schism. Faced with what he had experienced in Paris and Avignon, in contrast to how he presently lived far from these cities, Clamanges concluded his literary exile was the best way to serve the Church—and the safest, the historical observer might add with at least partially justified cynicism.[37]

THE FRUITS OF THE EREMITICAL LIFE

The various components of Clamanges' conception of the *reformatio personalis* come together in *De fructu heremi,* to which we have already referred, sent to Raoul de la Porte as he studied theology at the University of Paris. Writing in 1410 from his retreat at Fontaine-au-Bois, Clamanges once more built on his own experiences of a resuscitative and instructive *vita contemplativa* enjoyed after a disturbing, tumultuous *vita activa.* The treatise contains familiar themes: God's correction, the lessons of adversity, the roles of fear and humility, and the essential place of solitude as a palliative setting for the spiritual journey. What Clamanges did in *De fructu heremi,* however, was neatly tie these themes up in a manner that allows the student of his thought to understand more deeply how all of these parts contribute to the *reformatio personalis* and help to make the reform of the individual Christian the indispensable first step toward reforming the institutional Church.

Clamanges delineated the fruits of the eremitical life by appealing to

---

37. C 599.51–55 (L 2:247), following Lam 3:28; C 606.15–27 (L 2:250–51); C 171.27–30 (L 2:102), referring to Jerome, CSEL 54:1, 191 [Ep. 22.30]: "... *et tanto dehinc studio diuina legisse, quanto mortalia ante non legeram*"; C 497.19–27, 497.48–498.71 (L 2:296, 297); C 549.50–66 (L 1:78–79). Bernstein cited the reference to Jerome with the letter to Constance to illustrate his contention that during his active exiles Clamanges "believed he was experiencing something analogous to conversion": Bernstein, NP, 18–20.

his reader's scriptural background. Though never a Master of Theology himself, Clamanges skillfully used Old and New Testament examples to illustrate nearly every point, beginning with the benefits of purgative experiences in the desert. A central tenet for Clamanges was that God gives life to His people and teaches them to avoid excess in the desert. Clamanges quoted the Psalmist to say the believer sees God's sanctuary, power, and glory in the desert, which was like the land of milk and honey, that is, heaven. The way of the desert must not be impeded, however challenging. Rather, the Christian ought to embrace the penance, reconciliation, justice, and grace that are part of the desert experience and open heaven's gates. Through this purgation in the desert, the happy spirit will be freed from its carnal chains and merit eternal life. The way will be difficult but there is nothing to fear, Clamanges wrote; though there is no water in the desert, there is an abundance of faith that can move mountains. The Old Testament offered many examples of the faithful living profitably in the desert that Clamanges adopted to illustrate his points. Freed from their Egyptian enslavement, the Hebrews wandered in the desert for forty years before reaching Canaan; Moses stayed on Mt. Sinai for forty days while he fasted; David fled from Saul into the desert. During these periods, Clamanges pointed out, God did not abandon His people in the desert but supported them and showed them many signs of His glory, including providing water from a rock and setting out a column of fire to protect them.[38]

Clamanges in *De fructu heremi* complemented his Old Testament examples of desert experiences with desert events from Jesus' life, leaning once more on the *imitatio Christi* spirituality of his age that especially embraced Jesus' suffering. He described how Jesus was led by the Holy Spirit into the desert where He fasted and was tempted by the devil. A victor by way of this eremitical solitude, Christ emerged as the new Adam. Clamanges promised de la Porte that the world's allures cannot conquer the Christian who receives the aid of the angels as Jesus did in the desert; who is strengthened by Christ's love; and who follows His

38. B 2:28.64–67, 75–80 (L 1:122–23); B 2:31.149–52 (L 1:124), following 1 Sm 23:25, Tb 8:3; B 2:38.342–39.361 (L 1:128), following Nm 14:18 and 16:13, Dt 6:3 and 11:9, Jb 39:5, Pss 63:2–3 and 78:23, Acts 16:26; B 2:41.433–42.469 (L 1:129–30), following Jgs 18:10.

example. In fact, in his second reference to Christ's forty days in the desert, appended to the examples of the Hebrews' forty years of wandering and Moses' forty days on Mt. Sinai, Clamanges suggested Jesus specifically invites the Christian to imitate Him in His desert penance.[39]

Another result of the eremitical life in the desert was the fact that the spiritual fruits of the Holy Spirit would overcome the carnal fruits of the world, which men wrongly value. Clamanges explained the Spirit renews men of God and protects them from being tainted by the world. Using the examples of Jerome, Cassian, and Evagrius, Clamanges explained that the Spirit's fruits nurtured their minds instead of their stomachs. Insulating themselves from secular luxuries, the desert Fathers sought not to be praised as heroes but as beasts of solid mind and body. They succeeded by their labors, rigorous discipline, austere lives, and fasts. Rhetorically raising the objection it was easier to live a life of faith and austerity in the Fathers' era than in his own, Clamanges answered himself: God grants virtue in the present time just as He did in the past. Clamanges' use in *De fructu heremi* of the desert Fathers as examples to be imitated echoed the same point made over a decade earlier during his first active exile in Langres. In a letter to Montreuil pleading for moderation and railing against the greed of courtly life, Clamanges noted the fasting, frugality, and solitude of Egyptian confessors and anchorites led to admirable lives that conquered desires of the flesh.[40]

But even though Clamanges carefully described and admired the fruits of the life of the desert, he admitted in *De fructu heremi* this spiritual path is not always appreciated. The worst sinners often condemn the penance of the desert experience. To illustrate his point, he noted that the same Hebrews who had been helped by God in their forty years of wandering also complained and acted sinfully. Many even returned to Egypt; few persisted to achieve the goal of the promised land. To his distress, Clamanges found the same to be true in his day. In harsh terms he compared his contemporaries with the ungrateful Hebrews who were

39. B 2:29.81–89, 95–106 (L 1:123), following Mt 4:1–11, Mk 1:12–13, Lk 4:1–13; B 2:39.363–67 (L 1:128). Clamanges added one more New Testament desert example as a model for imitation apart from the life of Christ. The laboring woman clothed with the sun escapes into the desert to a place prepared by God: B 2:30.131–31.136 (L 1:124), following Rv 12:6.

40. B 2:32.172–33.215 (L 1:124–25); C 131.378–86 (L 2:78).

not content with what the Lord provided, noting they revert to their sinful ways as a dog returns to its vomit. Clamanges despaired anyone would follow his advice despite the presence of a torrent of evils and his examples of desert struggles as spiritual aids. Few people saw or even wished to see the heavenly reward. Those who had undertaken penance produced little fruit, scarcely persisted, and gave into the behaviors Clamanges fiercely lamented.[41]

Finally, Clamanges presented Scripture study as an antidote to help Christians who were wavering in their spiritual journey toward personal reform. Scripture and Christ's precepts, understood through the commentaries of the Fathers, teach the Christian not to turn from God and choose secular allures, but rather to condemn such errors. Reading and hearing Scripture helps the Christian understand and embrace the aid constantly being offered by the Holy Spirit in the eremitical life. Clamanges repeated this theme in his letter to the new Celestine when he identified Scripture as the font of human learning from which would flow the largess of heaven: virtue, wisdom, and a humble spirit.[42] Clamanges also discussed the preeminence of Scripture with the symbol of bread. Bread was frequently provided for the bodies of the faithful, as when Christ fed the five thousand. But the word of God is a more important food: as Jesus said when rejecting the devil during His temptation in the desert, Clamanges explained, man lives not by bread alone but by every word that comes from the mouth of God. While bread feeds the body, the word of God nourishes the spirit; thus fed, the Christian has no desire for fine appearances and is content with just a little bit of food. This reason explains why the hermit flees worldly banquets: he knows they are the way to ruin. Those who choose to lead the eremitical life and to live in the house of God instead of the tabernacle of sin should seek bread and meditate upon the yoke that does not burden. This bread is the word of God, which cannot be overcome.[43]

If God's word is the bread of the eremitical life, what fruits come

41. B 2:39.369–40.394 (L 1:128–29); B 2:44.507–509 (L 2:131), following Prv 26:11.

42. B 2:66.536–37 (L 1:142), following Rom 15:4; B 2:34.241–46 (L 1:126); B 2:29.92–95 (L 1:123); C 188.90–92, 95–98 (L 2:112).

43. B 2:43.480–93 (L 1:130), following Mt 14:13–21, Mk 6:34–44, Lk 9:10–17, Jn 6:1–13; B 2:44.500–515 (L 1:130–31), following Mt 4:4.

from eating the bread of meditation, according to Clamanges? These he reviewed in *De fructu heremi:* consolation; prayer that leads to dialogue with God; the study of Scripture that allows the reader to reach great heights, bear hardship, and avoid error; the reminder that one is never alone when one is with God; the exhortation that the Christian turn inward to the ways of the heart and away from sin; and the assurance that the contemplative Christian will be carried away from sin and up toward heaven. The eremitical life represents the challenge of the spiritual journey: to choose the way of God or the way of the world. Clamanges listed the results of following the world's ways as opposed to the eremitical path, that is, by allowing carnal desires to rule over the gifts of the Spirit. Laziness results in useless people; rebellion and insolence arise. Whoever serves the times increases in flattery and falsehood; following the public's ways adds dangers and pushes the Christian further from the life of virtue. But God, Clamanges continued, desires Christians to be free from the world's ways: He wants His children to renounce those earthly burdens in order to follow the example set by Christ. While some foolishly see the fruits of the world as sweeter, in truth they are not. Following Paul, Clamanges contended the foolishness of God is wiser than the wisdom of man: what is wise to the world is foolish to God. "Who wishes to be the friend of this world," Clamanges cited James, "is made the enemy of God." The friend of the eremitical life, by contrast, will have so reformed his personal life that the institutional reform Clamanges hoped would refocus the Church in head and members on pastoral care would have deep roots and achieve lasting results.[44]

DEVOTIONAL INFLUENCES

We may ask about the sources from which Clamanges drew his spiritual inspiration. Where did he get the ideas and images for his central theme of an eremitical *reformatio personalis* focused on the imitation of Christ? The effort can also help locate Clamanges in the devotional milieu of late medieval Europe when spirituality was characterized by an

44. B 2:34.222–41 (L 1:125–26); B 2:35.259–64 (L 1:126), following Lk 14:33; B 2:44.522–45.539 (L 1:131); B 2:45.544–55 (L 1:131), following 1 Cor 1:25, 2:14, 3:19; B 2:46.558 (L 1:131), following Jas 4:4.

emotional or affective approach that emphasized interiority. This interior focus urged a return to simplicity, purity, and inward spiritual growth as the bases for personal reform. Giles Constable sees an earlier influence: for him, late medieval theologians and humanists built on the twelfth century's emphasis on interiority, self-knowledge in solitude, the marriage of action and contemplation, and a basic identification of man's dignity with respect to God's image and Christ's humanity. The most obvious place to begin is Clamanges' reliance on personal and eremitical progress in the spiritual life as captured by the *imitatio Christi* tradition. Constable notes that in the late Middle Ages the act of imitating Christ followed patristic and earlier medieval concerns with the twin strands of Christ's humanity and divinity, but increasingly applied them to an everyday spirituality.[45]

Clamanges never wrote a full-scale version of the life of Christ complete with meditative suggestions, as did many of his contemporaries. One of the most important works produced during the late medieval period was the *Imitation of Christ,* attributed with persistent trepidation to Thomas à Kempis (1380–1471).[46] The idea has been advanced that Clamanges himself was the author of *Imitation.* This thesis, however, is unconvincing, since it is based on thematic and linguistic correlations between the *Imitation of Christ* and Clamanges' writings which may be found in the works of many other authors of the period. The claim has not drawn any attention and the thesis is itself highly qualified: "il est possible de montrer qu'*il n'est pas impossible* que Nicolas de Clamanges ait composé l'Imitation."[47] This fact, of course, does not preclude Cla-

45. Giles Constable, "Twelfth-Century Spirituality and the Late Middle Ages," *Medieval and Renaissance Studies* 5 (1971): 27–60, especially 32–36, and "The Popularity of Twelfth-Century Spiritual Writers in the Late Middle Ages," in *Renaissance Studies in Honor of Hans Baron,* ed. Anthony Molho and John A. Tedeschi (Dekalb, Ill.: Northern Illinois University Press, 1971), 5–28. Constable offers a comprehensive portrait of the *imitatio Christi* tradition in *Three Studies in Medieval Religious and Social Thought* (Cambridge: Cambridge University Press, 1995), 145–248.

46. John Van Engen, trans., *Devotio Moderna: Basic Writings* (New York: Paulist Press, 1988), 8–10, especially n. 5. Albert Ampe employed a codicological analysis to refute the attribution to Thomas à Kempis and speculated the author may have been a German Carthusian: Ampe, *L'Imitation de Jésus-Christ et son auteur. Réflexions critiques* (Rome: Edizioni di storia e letteratura, 1973), 42–56, 113–21.

47. A. Kwanten, "Nicolas de Clamanges et l'Imitation de Jésus-Christ," *Mémoires de la*

manges' adoption of the *imitatio Christi* tradition. Its influence on his
reform thought is obvious and a copy of the very popular *De vita Christiana* by Ludolf of Saxony (d. 1378) was in the library of the Collège de
Navarre at the University of Paris, Clamanges' intellectual home. His
classmate Jean Gerson recommended Ludolf's meditative treatise in the
context of personal and pastoral reform when he drew up a reading list
for bishops and pastors. Other near contemporaries, such as the author
of the *Meditationes vitae Christi* (ca. 1346–64), like Clamanges used the
imitation of Christ to convey a patristic emphasis on personal reform in
the context of late medieval institutional chaos. The author of the *Meditationes vitae Christi,* as did Ludolf and Clamanges, specifically urged
his readers to bear adversity with patience and humility, to suffer with
Christ, to emphasize prayer and asceticism within their own daily lives,
and to follow past examples of faith by contemplative meditation on
them before imitating their model in action.[48]

Despite the fact Clamanges did not write a *vita Christi* manual of
prayer, he turned to this theme several times in his writings, as we have
seen. His use of pious devotions centered around the imitation of Christ
indicates Clamanges was indeed drawing on the prevailing spiritual
trends of his age, especially as they were reflected and practiced by
adherents of the *devotio moderna.* Their founder, Geert Groote, probably
read Ludolf's *De vita Christiana* during his three-year stay at the Carthusian monastery at Monnikhuizen.[49] Since there is no explicit citation or

société d'agriculture, de commerce, des sciences et arts du department de la Marne 74 (1959):
91–100, especially 98 (original emphasis).

48. On the presence of Ludolf's work at Navarre, see Émile Chatelain, "Les manuscrits
du Collège de Navarre en 1741," *Revue des bibliothèques* 11 (1901): 371. Although Chatelain
reported the findings of a 1741 inventory, we know the Ludolf manuscript was in the Collège's library during Clamanges' era: Isabelle Chiavassa-Gouron, "Les lectures des maîtres
et étudiants du collège de Navarre: Un aspect de la vie intellectuelle à l'Université de Paris
(1380–1520)" (M.A. thesis, École Nationale des Chartes, 1985), 162; on Gerson's use of
Ludolf, see 107–108. Lawrence F. Hundersmarck offers a comparison of the *De vita Christiana* and the *Meditationes vitae Christi* in "Preaching the Passion: Late Medieval 'Lives of
Christ' as Sermon Vehicles," in *De Ore Domini: Preacher and Word in the Middle Ages,* ed.
Thomas L. Amos, Eugene A. Green, and Beverly Mayne Kienzle (Kalamazoo, Mich.:
Medieval Institute Publications, 1989), 147–167.

49. Hundersmarck sees Ludolf seeking a return to biblical, patristic, and monastic
piety linked to a *devotio moderna* spirituality that was "Christocentric, affective, moraliz-
ing, Scriptural, ascetic, and anti-speculative": "A Study of the Spiritual Themes in the

quotation of any *devotio moderna* author in Clamanges' writings, we cannot prove he was directly influenced by this tradition. But the movement
did flourish in northern Europe precisely at the time Clamanges studied
at Paris and enjoyed his active exiles. Clamanges' writings frequently
reflect the movement's emphases on individual reform, the imitation of
Christ, purgation, personal progress in the virtues, a private spiritual
journey, meditation on Scripture, and a reliance on the gifts of the Holy
Spirit. All of these elements of spirituality built upon the origins of
monasticism, which stressed an individual monk's personal reform. Clamanges would have been familiar with monastic practices and spiritual
goals through his long stays at the Augustinian monastery at Fontaine-
au-Bois during his second exile. His visits to the Carthusian monastery
of Valprofonde during this period brought him into direct contact with
the affective, eremitical, and interior piety that reflects the order's contemplative and silence-centered spirituality, a spirituality infusing the *De
vita Christiana* of Ludolf of Saxony, one of their own. This visit mirrored
Groote's retreat with the Carthusians at Monnikhuizen where he
embraced contemplation, but not to the exclusion of action as a necessary part of living a Christian life. Groote read, purchased, and recommended the Fathers from Cassian to Bernard, especially regarding the
monastic *vita contemplativa* and resulting action. Groote's first disciple,
Geert Zerbolt, emphasized inner knowledge led to spiritual growth
when it was grounded in penitence, self-mortification, humility, obedience, fear, and silence in imitation of Christ's example.[50]

Prayers and Passion Narration of Ludolphus de Saxonia's *Vita Jesu Christi"* (Ph.D. diss.,
Fordham University, 1983), 34, 36. On Groote's reading of Ludolf at Monnikhuizen, see
History of the Church, ed. Hubert Jedin and John Dolan (New York: Crossroad, 1982),
4:427.

50. Van Engen, *Devotio Moderna: Basic Writings,* complements and updates R. R. Post,
The Modern Devotion (Leiden: E. J. Brill, 1968). See also Gründler, *"Devotio Moderna
Atque Antiqua:* The Modern Devotion and Carthusian Spirituality," in *The Spirituality of
Western Christendom,* vol. 2, *The Roots of the Modern Christian Tradition,* ed. E. Rozanne
Elder (Kalamazoo, Mich.: Cistercian Publications, 1984), 27–45. Steven Ozment notes
Clamanges was fundamentally in line with the northern European piety of the *devotio
moderna*: *The Age of Reform 1250–1550: An Intellectual and Religious History of Late Medieval
and Reformation Europe* (New Haven: Yale University Press, 1980), 79.

The only work by Groote we can track with which Clamanges could have come into
contact is a letter Groote wrote on the topic of priests with concubines. This letter is listed

The influence of the Fathers and Carthusian spirituality on the *devotio moderna* and Clamanges is implicit, although in *De fructu heremi* Clamanges explicitly referred to the religious practices of the Carthusians when recommending the renunciation of worldliness with the embrace of penance and prayer. But like Groote and his followers, Clamanges took personal reform one step further than the Carthusians. He moved beyond the *contemptus mundi,* progressing from the solitary contemplative life to the active life of faith and service—following Christ in both prayer and action, in word and deed. As Clamanges wrote in *De fructu heremi,* was it not better to join with friends in a pleasant, communal life as well as to work for salvation in the world?[51] Adherents of the *devotio moderna* likewise built on prayer, performing works of charity and mercy as part of their personal reform. An active life was treated as the natural result of a contemplative life. This idea of a *vita mixta* would not have rung falsely with Clamanges. He shifted between the *vita contemplativa* and the *vita activa* during the alternating periods of his public service and private retreats. He was drawn to the ascetical life as much by a natural disposition as he was pushed there by political circumstances. Clamanges learned the value of adversity though his own experiences, which he transformed into a rhetorical call for personal reform via the imitation of Christ. Clamanges drew on the spiritual milieu of his age not only as devotional exercises, but as a tool to encourage a life of faith and constant personal reform. Once properly focused on his personal reform, the Christian could move from interior spiritual progress to reforming the institutional Church in her head and members.

---

as part of Benedict XIII's traveling library (ca. 1405–8) in Marie-Henriette Jullien de Pommerol and Jacques Monfrin, *La bibliothèque pontificale à Avignon et à Peniscola pendant le Grand Schisme d'Occident et sa dispersion. Inventaires et concordances* (Rome: École Française de Rome, 1991), 173.

51. B 2:35.267–36.280 (L 1:126). On monasticism as the best way to achieve personal reform, see Ladner, *The Idea of Reform,* 319–40.

CHAPTER 4

Pastoral Reform in Head and Members

❧❧

Clamanges' fundamental concern with institutional reform in head and members was directed toward the *cura animarum* of the faithful, which he saw as the central responsibility of every cleric from the highest echelons of the ecclesiastical hierarchy down to the local parish level. Like virtually every other reformer of his era, Clamanges was concerned with the reform of the institutional Church *in capite et in membris,* in head and members.[1] As with inner and institutional reform, it is improper to separate the Church's head from her members, since they form an organic whole. Problems in one part of the body exacerbated problems in the others. This was especially true of the benefice system. As the late medieval economy imploded and the Schism persisted, competition for offices (including those with *cura animarum*) increased not only because two and then three popes offered patronage, but also because rarely could one benefice provide a sufficient livelihood. The Schism at the Church's head contributed to this and other pastoral problems *in membris,* leading to more diffuse attempts to address them on the local level. The urgency for pastoral reform of the head and members increased over time, as did the recognition of the parts' integral relationship with each other and the Church's head.[2]

1. The phrase had its origins in the canonical relationship between a cathedral chapter and its head, the bishop. It first appeared in a 1206 decretal of Innocent III and was applied by Nicholas IV to Cluniac reform. The phrase made its first conciliar appearance at Vienne in 1311 through William Durant the Younger, who used it in a proposal concerning the legal relationship between pope and bishops as well as the need for the pope to provide leadership in reform. See Stump, *Reforms,* 237–39; for a comprehensive treatment, see Karl Augustin Frech, *Reform an Haupt und Gliedern: Untersuchungen zur Entwicklung und Verwendung der Formulierung im Hoch- und Spätmittelalter* (Frankfurt: Peter Lang, 1992).

2. Johannes Helmrath, "Reform als Thema der Konzilien des Spätmittelalters," in *Christian Unity: The Council of Ferrara-Florence 1438/9–1989,* ed. Giuseppe Alberigo (Leuven: Leuven University Press, 1991), 84–90.

91

The Church's head was sometimes defined as consisting of both the pope and the college of cardinals whose members declared they were *pars corporis papae*. Cardinals saw themselves as key elements of the Roman church and indeed Clamanges specifically targeted them for failing to provide exemplary leadership *in capite*. This head also included curial bishops.[3] It is with these parties in mind—pope, cardinals, and curial bishops—that Clamanges spoke of the reform of the Church's head, particularly when criticizing the large bureaucracy that had become the hallmark of the Avignon curia. Clamanges sought a *reformatio in capite* primarily because he wanted the pope, cardinals, and curial bishops to provide proper examples of pastoral care for diocesan ordinaries and priests. His reform program, however, was not strictly or simply the top-down program of Gerson and others. They moved from the ineffective French subtractions of obedience through the disaster of Pisa to Constance by progressively concentrating on reform *in capite*. For them, comprehensive reform must begin at the top and then trickle down to produce a corresponding reform *in membris*.[4] Clamanges indeed saw problems in the head of the Church trickling down to exacerbate similar problems in her members. The solution to these prob-

3. Brian Tierney, *Foundations of the Conciliar Theory* (Cambridge: Cambridge University Press, 1955), 68–84, treats the canonical background of the Roman church and the relationship between the college of cardinals and the papacy. See also Tierney, "Hostiensis and Collegiality," in *Proceedings of the Fourth International Congress of Medieval Canon Law*, ed. Stephan Kuttner (Vatican City: Biblioteca Apostolica Vaticana, 1976), 401–9; Joseph Lecler, "*Pars corporis papae*—le Sacré Collège dans l'ecclésiologie médiévale," in *L'homme devant Dieu: Mélanges offerts au Père Henri de Lubac* (Paris: Aubier, 1964), 2:183–98, and "Le cardinalat de l'Église romaine: son évolution dans l'histoire," *Études* 330 (1969): 871–79.

4. Although focusing on hierarchical reform, Gerson was also devoted to the religious lives of the parish laity, as D. Catherine Brown demonstrated in *Pastor and Laity in the Theology of Jean Gerson* (Cambridge: Cambridge University Press, 1987). According to Mark S. Burrows, *Jean Gerson and De Consolatione Theologiae (1418): The Consolation of a Biblical and Reforming Theology for a Disordered Age* (Tübingen: J. C. B. Mohr [Paul Siebeck], 1991), Gerson held that all of the faithful and not just theologians, as Aquinas believed, should have an explicit understanding of the faith (108–14). He uses Gerson's position to demonstrate his "anti-elitism" (219–21) and a "populist approach to theology" that led Burrows to identify this treatise "as offering in programmatic terms a 'democratization' of theology" (144). But, as Burrows points out, while Gerson was deeply concerned with the laity, he consistently looked to a top-down program of reform even while his faith it could succeed waned (256–63).

lems, however, did not flow exclusively from the top. The *reformatio in capite* was ultimately aimed in support of the reform of pastoral care that was to be in progress *in membris* already. For Clamanges, the reform *in capite* could never be divorced from the reform *in membris*. Neither could be seen apart from the indispensable personal reform that would lead to improvements in pastoral care.

Clamanges over time turned to the reform of the entire Church, noting in one of his letters to Constance that the *Ecclesia* was comprised of prelates, priests, various ministers, secular authorities, and all of the faithful acting with religious devotion.[5] The Church *in membris,* for Clamanges, was comprised of the body of the faithful, parish priests, and diocesan bishops, responsible overall for the *cura animarum* of their sees. As Trent would legislate over a century later, Clamanges stressed diocesan bishops were especially charged with exercising their pastoral duty by ordaining worthy candidates to the priesthood and by making sure parish priests set good examples and cared properly for their flocks. Clamanges discussed bishops in connection with reform *in capite* and *in membris* because of their roles connecting the head with the body of the Church.

Clamanges' plan for far-reaching pastoral reform may be seen in two major parts. The first, which was more Clamanges' focus in the initial stages of his career, began by describing the corruption of the Church *in capite*, which set bad moral examples. He discussed in detail the problems that commonly plagued this part of the Church—especially simony, worldly ambition, and hypocrisy—paying particular attention to the Avignon curia and college of cardinals. Clamanges then demonstrated what should be papal and episcopal examples of pastoral service by contrasting the ideal of shepherds conscientiously leading their flocks with the lamentable reality of shepherds who completely ignored them. The second major part centered on the failure of pastoral care and the need for reform *in membris,* topics that he increasingly addressed at length in treatises and letters from the latter stages of his career. He took care to illustrate how the problems of the Church's head aggravated troubles in her members. A particularly troubling manifestation of pastoral failure

5. C 488.68–76 (L 2:291).

occurred when the *cura animarum* was left to untrained mercenaries. Such so-called pastors led the faithful astray through their ignorance and immorality while the proper holders of benefices enjoyed multiple incomes far from their parishes. Often parishioners were more like sheep surrounded by wolves: the priests or poor substitutes charged with watching over, not despoiling, their own flocks.

THE REFORM *in capite*

Clamanges emphasized that when the clergy *in capite* neglected the *cura animarum,* their negligence had a negative impact upon pastoral care in the Church's members. Clamanges had used this imagery of a damaged head harming its members when describing how the French subtraction of obedience from the Avignon papacy also adversely affected the French clergy and faithful. He returned to this imagery as the Schism wore on. Concluding a letter to Nicolas de Baye written from Fontaine-au-Bois in late 1414 or January 1415 when the general council of Constance was beginning its deliberations, Clamanges called for a reform in the head and members of a Church beset by abuse, error, and weakness, as well as for a return to the discipline, zeal, and devotion of the ancient Church.[6] The relation between head and members was also made clear in several 1414 letters to Reginald, bishop of Soissons, in which Clamanges described the bishop's major role as an exemplar of service; the prince and the bishop's responsibility to care for those entrusted to them; and the importance of preserving the entire public good. He described the dangerous consequences for the faithful when bishops abdicated their pastoral responsibilities and lived the kind of secular life they ought properly to condemn. Clamanges returned to vegetative imagery to make his point that when bishops acted in this manner, the entire Church suffered. Like a neglected garden, the Church withered and could not grow without the water that made her fertile: the teaching of salvation that helped her to flourish.[7]

6. C 494.271–76 (L 2:294): *"Reformabitur Ecclesia universa, in capite ac membris singulis incredibiliter labefactata, corrigentur errores, comprimentur excessus, abusus auferentur, florebit iustitia, resurget disciplina, zelus, devotio antiqua, gravitas atque honestas ad priscum morem reparabuntur."*
7. C 622.92–623.113 (L 2:340), especially 92–100: *"Prelatori[u]m autem litteratorumque virorum officium fuerat hanc vitam dampnare, hos mores effeminatissimos constanter ac perse-*

The central problem at the head of the Church to Clamanges' eyes was the greed that spread many evils throughout her members. Greed particularly led to simony and moral blindness, producing a papacy and curia with no concern for others. Because of greed, pastoral care was simply not on the agenda of the Church, starting with its highest point. Clamanges argued in *De ruina,* as he had done when opposing the withdrawal of obedience, that Avignon prelates failed to see how their greed and neglect produced ruin for themselves, for all in the Church, and for the entire order of state and society.[8] Greed in the Church was manifested most often where benefices were involved, leading Clamanges to write frequently against simony in his letters and especially in his 1412 treatise *Contra prelatos symoniacos.* There he identified simony as the root of all the Church's rampant problems: vices, lack of devotion among the faithful, secular encroachments on ecclesiastical liberty, dangers and abuses of dishonorable, unworthy ministers.[9]

Simony and its consequent neglect of the *cura animarum* within the ecclesiastical hierarchy troubled Clamanges early in his career, especially when he witnessed these practices as Benedict XIII's secretary from November 1397 to June 1398. In a letter written in the summer of 1398 to

---

veranter arguere, monstrare pericula ex his nasci solita: lapsus politiarum, ruinas urbium, mortes principum, clades regnorum. Sed proh dolor!—pontifices nostri ceterique in ecclesiasticis gradibus instituti non tam principes in rebus istis reprehendere quam plausibiliter assentari, et quodammodo imitari, sunt soliti.* See also C 624.163–72 (L 2:341), following Is 15:6, Sg 4:15, Is 1:30.

8. C 365.191–99 (L 2:223): *"Inde oritur ruina Ecclesie, labes morum, sentina viciorum, vite spurcitia, iniquitatis abundantia, caritatis refrigerium, fidei periclitatio, errorum pullulatio, religionis exinanitio, scismatis pestilentissimi virus exitiale, sacerdotii denique totiusque ordinis ecclesiastici contemptus atque opprobrium et despicabilis ignominia, que nemo utique mirabitur, qui didicerit necesse esse ex corruptis et male sanis capitibus male sanos sensus ac motus vitalesque spiritus in cetera membra diffundi."* See also Coville, *Le Traité,* 148. Clamanges' early concern with prelates' failure to see their own faults and the consequences of their greed is also found in a 1395 letter: C 18.112–62 (L 2:12–13); C 25.385–90 (L 2:17).

9. B 2:145.267–75, 2:146.306–147.309 (L 1:164, 165): *"Ex hac autem peste capitalissima tota surgit Ecclesie desolatio, tota quam in ea cernimus abhominatio. Ex hoc fonte omnes plage, oppressio, persecutio, contemptus ac vilipensio et, vt vno absoluam uerbo, omnia in eam mala profluunt. Vnde enim plebis indeuotio, sacerdotum inhonoratio, libertatis exinanitio, tributorum prestatio, iurium ecclesiasticorum per secularem potestatem occupatio, nisi quia vilissimis personis suoque gradu ac ministerio indignissimis plena est? . . . Quid me cetera oportet persequi ecclesiasticorum vicia grandia et incredibiliter enormia ex hac radice corruptissima pullulantia, que, vt non dicam meo, vix vllo satis explicari possent eloquio?"*

Benedict XIII, Clamanges condemned curialists in Avignon who arrogantly indulged their greed, listened only to themselves, and persecuted others. Clamanges referred to the vices at Avignon, and expressed his joy at escaping them, in a letter to Jean de Montreuil written shortly after he arrived in Langres. The Avignon papal curia was as worldly as a princely court: greed, luxury, arrogance, and ambition ran rampant. Living there was as dangerous as navigating through Scylla and Charybdis. There was no spiritual peace, faith, or charity; duplicity and flattery reigned as the wheel of fortune spun. Clamanges at this time complained to Gerson and d'Ailly about the simony he had seen that led to pluralism, absenteeism, and the misappropriation of funds for private use instead of parochial service. Clamanges bluntly charged greedy curialists with distancing themselves from the *cura animarum* associated with their benefices. Concerned more with luxury and vices, they were distracted from spiritual matters and their pastoral duties.[10]

Clamanges took central aim at this problem *in capite* when he complained during the early part of his career that prelates sought only more money, not to serve God. Just under one half of *De ruina* was concerned with discussing and criticizing the financial abuses of the Church in her uppermost levels, where the care of souls was sacrificed for curial greed. Ambitious, avaricious prelates set bad examples, seeking only to serve themselves by gaining the status and money of offices instead of serving the Church through the exercise of their benefices. He harshly condemned those who took advantage of their simple-minded flocks by cheating, threatening, and taxing them heavily. The situation was so bad, Clamanges commented sardonically, prelates' concern for themselves may have provided an unintended benefit: because they held so

10. C 85.95–103 (L 2:52); C 94.11–95.66 (L 2:57–58); C 95.71–96.87 (L 2:58). In another letter to Benedict four years earlier, Clamanges had complained clerics were led astray by their blind ambition: C 8.43–48 (L 2:6–7). For the letter to d'Ailly, see C 177.73–83 (L 2:105): "*Ex habundantia enim temporalium nata superbia est, ex fastu superbie orta ambitio, ex fructibus ambitionis ocium profectum. Ex ineriti autem ocio prodiit luxuria, quibus rebus ita a sua primeva institutione a curaque et exercitio rerum spiritualium in vanitates et insanias falsas delapsa est, ut iam irrisioni habeantur, qui non cum ceteris in talibus insaniant. Nonne autem utilius est temporaliter ad eruditionem disciplinamque flagellari, quam ocio, luxu, vanitate ceterorumque viciorum exuberantia spiritualiter et fortassis eternaliter deperire?*" Clamanges made similar comments in a contemporary letter to Gerson: C 183.89–184.148 (L 2:109–10).

many benefices, they were almost always absent and so could not harm the churches ostensibly placed in their care.

Particularly disturbing to Clamanges, who noted often he had witnessed these abuses himself at Avignon, was the fact that curial bishops were among the worst offenders in terms of being worldly and far from the care of their flocks. The curia, full of vice, was a haven for simony not only within the circle of papal patronage but also when prelates negotiated with secular princes to fill benefices. In turn, secular princes conspired with curial officials to control benefices or to support the cardinals' candidates, sometimes even over the pope's choices. Curial bishops knew more of worldly matters than divine, making deals with secular princes to further their private ambitions instead of the Church's pastoral interests, despite their appearance of laudable public service. He charged these curial bishops with being unlettered, immoral, and full of vices. They were, in fact, bishops in name only: they never visited their dioceses except to plunder them and cared nothing for the spiritual state of their flocks.

The papacy and curia were so involved in greed, Clamanges declared, scarcely one prelate in a thousand was honorable. He detailed his complaints against specific excesses and problems: rigged elections, reservations, vacancies, annates, spolia, collects, expectancies, and the strict collection of taxes. These excesses resulted in money flowing from all over Europe into the apostolic camera and the abuse of excommunication as a threat to force payment. Corrupt litigation was also common in the curia: gold bought justice, so the poor often lost to the rich when petitioning for benefices. Rules were frequently manipulated to help the chancery make money by keeping disputes unsettled and ongoing. There were now more robbers than true pastors in the curia, a house of prayer that had been turned into a den of thieves. Clamanges even speculated with sarcasm that a prelate who decided to abandon greed would be attacked by his colleagues, be declared unworthy of the priesthood, and be deprived of his benefices by others who knew better than he the tricks of gaining offices and fees.[11]

---

11. Coville, *Le Traité*, 115–22, 125–30, 131–35, 145. In *Contra prelatos symoniacos,* Clamanges observed that often the poor could not even compete for offices: B 2:141.142–43 (L 1:162).

Clamanges especially criticized the college of cardinals at Avignon in *De ruina:* cardinals personified curial artifice, arrogance, and greed. They abolished free canonical elections and appointed incompetents to benefices in order to control the offices and to appropriate the funds connected to them. Theirs were the worst excesses of pluralism and absenteeism: the cardinals grabbed for every vacant benefice regardless of the income and used any trick available to them. Although he claimed the cardinals' crimes were so vast it would take Cicero to describe them, Clamanges continued in Ciceronian fashion to pass over repeatedly *("Transeo . . . transeo . . . transeo . . .")* the excesses he then listed: simony, corruption, abuse of judicial proceedings, usury. Cardinals were Pharisees who did not do anything to lift the burdens they had placed on the Church. Like the Pharisees, cardinals especially delighted in their phylacteries, long robes, and titles. Writing in 1408 from Valprofonde after he left Benedict XIII's service for the second time, Clamanges repeated his earlier complaints that ecclesiastics in high places acted with feigned zeal for the Church and produced only troubles through their selfishness. He also criticized the keeping of concubines, which he feared was all too common a practice; he charged that prelates permitted priests to keep concubines and engage in other sexual sins with impunity. Clamanges continually criticized the curialists' desires to serve man instead of God, as in his bold 1398 letter to Benedict XIII where he twice reminded the Avignon pope that all who served in the Church must obey God, not man. A few years later in *De ruina* Clamanges described curialists as mercenaries in the king's pay who ignored the care of their flocks.[12]

Despite this litany of financial and moral abuses *in capite,* Clamanges never ceased to maintain popes and bishops should provide examples of leadership, morality, and dedicated pastoral service. He generally praised Avignon's Benedict XIII and urged him to take a leading role in steering the ship of the Church to safety in storm-tossed seas and to fulfill his function as chief pastor of God's flock. In his self-serving 1394 letter to

12. Coville, *Le Traité,* 118, 122–26, 130, 133–34; C 612.135–613.145 (L 2:153); B 2:141.151–57 (L 1:162); B 2:146.299–305 (L 1:165); C 84.69–77 (L 2:52), following Acts 5:29; C 92.357–60 (L 2:56), following Pss 146:3, 118:8; C 610.31–37 (L 2:151). In *Contra prelatos symoniacos,* Clamanges again employed the Ciceronian style of rhetorically passing over *("pretereo," "taceo")* sexual abuses he then named.

Benedict, sent shortly after his election, Clamanges stated he did not believe the new pope preferred worldly pomp and pride to selfless service nor that he would be a slave to sin. Four years later, however, while Clamanges noted in a private letter to Montreuil his gratitude to Benedict XIII for sending him to Langres, he also pointed out the pope had been permitting the secular spirit of greed to reign in his curia. Still, in 1400–1401, Clamanges expressed some respect for the Avignon pope in his more public treatise *De ruina,* considering him better than his predecessors and, in a reversal, complementing him for not getting caught up in secular affairs or lawsuits. But Clamanges increasingly turned to bishops as the instruments for Church reform, especially after he definitively left Benedict XIII's service in 1408. Like Gerson, Clamanges relied on bishops to be exemplars and supervisors of pastoral ministry. Although this development in Clamanges' thought was certainly a result of his disillusionment and personal trouble with curial politics, it also reflects the tendency of reform councils to see the diocesan bishop as the key agent of reform tying the Church's head with her members. In emphasizing episcopal action, Clamanges continued this tradition of the Lateran councils, especially Lateran IV, a tradition that would receive a major revival at Trent over a century after his death.[13]

Clamanges' depiction of the bishop as the key agent of reform is clear from his 1414 letter to Reginald, bishop of Soissons, which he devoted to the episcopal roles of leader, pastor, and exemplar. He assured Reginald he was a pillar of the Church made strong by the Lord and an angel sent to spread God's word. Following Paul's mandate to Timothy, Clamanges instructed Reginald to teach, preach, aid, and correct those under him. The true pastor, he continued didactically, cares for his sheep and does not seize his flock's wool and milk. But not every bishop fulfilled his episcopal duties. Many French prelates, like secular princes, were led astray by luxury, neglected their tasks, and languished in vice. Prelates must argue constantly against profligate lives and point out the danger-

---

13. C 11.152–63 (L 2:8), following Jn 8:34, 2 Pt 2:19; C 95.62–65 (L 2:58); Coville, *Le Traité,* 144–45. On Gerson's treatment of episcopal leadership in reform, see Pascoe, *Jean Gerson,* 110–45. Gerson directed bishops to provide good examples and oversee pastoral duties by visitation; he even drafted an investigatory checklist: Brown, *Pastor and Laity,* 52–55, 72–73.

ous results of immorality, which Clamanges grandly identified as the destruction of societies. In contrast, bishops not only failed to rebuke princely lives of vice, they assented to and even imitated their immorality, much to Clamanges' chagrin. This subject of curial shepherds acting in an untrustworthy manner may also be noted several times throughout *De ruina*. Clamanges charged there that cardinals and bishops abandoned their flocks, simply ignored their pastoral work, and thereby disturbed pastoral bliss.[14]

An illustrative example of the dichotomy between what bishops ought charitably to do and what actions they in fact selfishly took is found in a passage from the letter to Reginald concerning largess. Clamanges declared the true fruit of riches to lie not in their possession but in their free distribution. However, bishops hoarded church funds that should properly be given to the poor, to whom they belonged. In *De ruina*, Clamanges had earlier turned to the early Church to provide a standard. The Fathers gave away the money their holiness attracted. With this money they established schools, churches, monasteries, and convents.[15] Ironically, their example of poverty, simplicity, and charity

---

14. C 621.23–55 (L 2:339–40), following Ps 75:4, Rv 3:12, Mal 2:7. Note the directness at C 622.56–66 (L 2:340): *"Sane, aut me hactenus erronea de [te] fefellit opinio aut ad ea, que pastoris sunt, docte, strenue, prudenter et laudabiliter exequenda singulari quadam es aptitudine instructus. Quare ista, rogo, de cetero fracti et pusilli animi verba omitte strenueque ad opus tuum accingere: precida, doce, exhortare, argue, obsecra, increpa in omni patientia et doctrina* (2 Tm 4:2). *Sanos confove, egr[o]tos sana, errantes revoca, rebelles corripe, contumaces plecti, i[gn]aros erudi, tepentes accende, tardos stimula, ardentes cohibe, negligentes obiurga."* C 622.69–623.113 (L 2:340–41); C 624.153–56 (L 2:341): *"Quis in universo regno illo pastor est, nisi forsitan tu ille es, qui gregem suum pascere curet aut etiam noverit, immo qui lana et lacte non assidue spoliat?"* C 624.172–625.179 (L 2:341); Coville, *Le Traité,* 117–18, 122, 129–32, 135.

15. C 624.139–41, 143–53 (L 2:341). See especially Coville, *Le Traité,* 113: *"Cernentes etenim seculares homines tam principes quam alii locupletes ejusmodi virorum Dei sanctam et sinceram conversacionem ab omni terrena fece igne divini amoris excoctam, certabant undique, illis quamvis renitentibus, bona copiosissima congerere, ut, ab omni cura soluti, fervori possent devocionis absque interrupcione, liberius incumbere, . . . sic denique omnes gradus universeque professiones hominum ecclesiasticorum militancium in amplissimas copias excreverunt, quas primitivi, illi patres qui suis eas acquisierant virtutibus, in prophanis usibus, quemadmodum nunc plerique, consumpserunt; sed aut in elemosinis et hospitalitate ceterisque caritatis ac pietatis operibus impendebant, aut si quis istis operibus menseque sue frugali supererat, in cellas edificandas, si fortassis alii fratres celitus inspirati religionis gracia advenissent inque alia paranda, quibus parandis opus erat, convertebant."*

Canon law did not grant ownership of church property or any connected revenues to priests or bishops; these belonged to God and were administered by clergy as trustees.

increased endowments, leading to the negative consequences of prosperity for the whole Church against which we have already heard Clamanges warn in terms of individual spiritual growth.[16] What these failures meant for shepherds and their sheep must now be explored in order to comprehend more fully how Clamanges' criticisms of the Church's head were designed to spur the reform of pastoral care throughout her body.

THE REFORM *in membris*

Clamanges devoted much attention during the early part of his career to the reform of the Church *in capite*, yet he increasingly concentrated on his ultimate reform goal: the pastoral care of Christians *in membris*. It is crucial to recall that Clamanges was concerned with simony and other problems *in capite* not primarily because he thought the head of the Church should be reformed *in se* but, more importantly for him, because the problems of the head exacerbated troubles throughout the entire body of the Church. Were Clamanges' complaints unique and was he demonstrating animosity toward the parochial clergy? *Devotio moderna* scholar John Van Engen notes Geert Groote voiced similar complaints against the local clergy and like his near contemporary Clamanges also used the word "ruin" to describe the current state of the Church. Van Engen posits it may not be accurate to characterize the *devotio moderna* as anticlerical, a nineteenth-century term with which late medieval critics including Groote and Clamanges would have been unfamiliar despite their agreement of the need for clerical reform.

According to the Fathers, church property was the patrimony of the poor. Innocent IV declared that the whole community of Christians owned the physical things of the Church; the poor had the right to be supported by such things or their revenues. See Tierney, *Medieval Poor Law* (Berkeley: University of California Press, 1959), 39–44.

16. Coville, *Le Traité*, 114, 115: *"Ubi vero, ut fere assolet, paulatim ex diviciis rerumque secundarum affluencia fluxus et insolencia in Ecclesiam subiere, tepescere sensim cepit religio, virtus hebescere, solvi disciplina, caritas minui, tolli humilitas, paupertas opprobrio esse simulque parsimonia, sed ut pompis et luxui res subesset, avaricia crescere que, non suis diu contenta finibus, aliena non modo ambire, sed rapere et invadere, inferiores opprimer et tam jure quam injuria spoliare. . . . Hanc enim diviciarum naturam novimus, ut quo uberius habentur, eo habentis animi ad sui semper incrementum majori accendere soleant concupiscencia. Ita igitur factum est paulatim, extincto cordibus eorum spiritu, frigescente caritate, tepente devocione, Deo oblito solis terremis fructibus capessendis inhyarent, sola in dignitatibus beneficiisque aliis emolumenta pensarent."*

Rather, the movement set high standards for priests as they justifiably singled out for censure the clergy's blatant shortcomings. Groote specifically protested against benefices that were stockpiled, vows that were broken, and priests who studied for worldly and personal profit instead of spiritual gain and pastoral service.[17] So, too, Clamanges' complaints and ideas about the local clergy reveal he was very much in line with late medieval complaints against the Church *in membris*. Clamanges was neither radical nor anticlerical, but merely exercising his self-defined role by pointing out for correction common clerical practices requiring reform.

Over time, Clamanges became more focused on the need for reform *in membris* and its impact on the Christian faithful. Many of the points he made at length in later letters and treatises on diocesan bishops and priests echoed earlier complaints against the papacy, curia, and cardinals, as did his didactic use of the imagery of the good and bad shepherds. Clamanges applied these problems to the Church *in membris* with growing frequency. We must consider, then, what Clamanges identified as the common problems in the local Church that drew parish priests away from their pastoral duties. The exploration of this topic, one of great importance for the reform thought of Clamanges, begins with a close look at his central work on the question of simony, *Contra prelatos symoniacos*. This treatise, addressed to Gerson in 1412, was not concerned with simony among cardinals and curial bishops, as was generally the case in *De ruina* and Clamanges' earlier letters on the topic. Clamanges dealt in *Contra prelatos symoniacos* on a more local level with diocesan bishops and parish priests, discussing especially the latter's moral examples, preaching, and their impact on their flocks.

From the first sentence of *Contra prelatos symoniacos*, Clamanges declared many greedy bishops in the Church were worthy of censure because they accepted money to ordain priests, even resorting to extor-

17. John Van Engen, "Late Medieval Anticlericalism: The Case of the New Devout," in *Anticlericalism in Late Medieval and Early Modern Europe*, ed. Peter A. Dykema and Heiko A. Oberman (Leiden: E. J. Brill, 1993), 19–52, especially 22–29. Elsewhere Groote again described the Church as being in ruin, this time adding that illness in the Church's head was the sympton of a grave disease whose fever ravaged her body: see G. Bonet-Maury, *Gérard de Groote, un précurseur de la réforme* (Paris: Librairie Sandoz et Fischbacher, 1878), 38–39.

tion. He described these bishops as no better than Simon Magus. Their actions were especially troubling: while all priests could administer the sacraments and preach, the distinguishing characteristic of the bishop's office was to ordain and assign priests to diocesan pastoral service. How terrible, he declared, that bishops failed to perform this distinctive episcopal role freely and instead acted in a greedy, worldly manner. Clamanges also refused to allow bishops who sold ordinations to excuse themselves: he denied their claims that the money they received was simply fitting payment for documentation. Bishops, Clamanges charged, went too far by refusing to allow the ordained to serve unless they had paid for the proper documents. It was only a ploy they used, unsuccessfully according to Clamanges, to hide their chicanery and greed.[18]

Priests buying ordination and benefices were just as culpable as the bishops selling them. Again turning to Simon Magus as a negative exemplar, he contended it was as offensive and simoniacal to buy an office as to sell one. Simoniacal buyers and sellers sometimes contended they were simply following the examples of others or local customs, thereby explaining away their own culpability. Clamanges countered the norm of divine law as interpreted by synodal decrees and explained by the Fathers, in addition to the good practices of justice and honesty, negated this excuse.[19] Clamanges even seemed to question the validity of simoniacal clerics' services. In *De ruina,* he sounded like a Donatist by implying sacramental grace was not conferred by a simoniacal cleric. This contention was repeated a decade later in *Contra prelatos symoniacos* when Clamanges quoted Gratian to question whether the grace of the Holy Spirit was conferred when money was exchanged. Later in the same text, he retreated from this implied charge: using Gratian once more, Clamanges noted even heretics may baptize.[20] He also sealed his condemna-

18. B 2:136.3–14 (L 1:160), following Acts 8:9–23; B 2:141.162–142.190 (L 1:163); B 2:144.239–145.253, 2:145.264–66 (L 1:164). Gerson, writing against simony, declared fees for sacraments, including ordination to priesthood, to be acceptable if they were reasonable: Pascoe, *Jean Gerson,* 132–33, and Brown, *Pastor and Laity,* 53.

19. B 2:137.28–31 (L 1:160), following Acts 8:18–20; B 2:143.197–210 (L 1:163); B 2:143.219–144.226 (L 1:164).

20. Coville, *Le Traité,* 130: *"Illud vero quomodo ferendum quod sacramenta, quibus nichil spiritualius est, palam veniunt, quod nullus ad clericatum vel ad sacrum ordinem vel ad quemcumque gradum ecclesiasticum nisi mercede accedit, quod nulli sacramentalem graciam requirenti manus imponunt, nisi qui certum antea precium dederit, quod omnes confessiones,*

tion of simony with lively images, as when he identified those involved in buying and selling benefices with the doomed son of perdition. The benefice market was so advanced and commonplace that he described his age as one of confusion, having the worst greed for gold. In the contemporary Church, quite far from the norm of the *ecclesia primitiva,* simony represented a golden gate for the ambitious and greedy. At the conclusion of *Contra prelatos symoniacos,* Clamanges asked Christ directly for help in rooting out simony, likening all buyers and sellers of Church offices to public merchants, even prostitutes, whose actions resulted in spiritual fornication.[21]

Simony led to other abuses *in membris* that Clamanges had also condemned *in capite.* One was the pluralism by which priests collected offices in imitation of avaricious cardinals above them in the hierarchy. All offices were bought regardless of size, income, or importance by greedy men who were more robbers than priests. He echoed a point he had made over a decade earlier in *De ruina* that there were more thieves than prayerful pastors in the curia. The rush for more benefices was especially strong when there was a new pope. Clerics who were not content with their present benefices—nor fit to serve the Church in any capacity, for that matter—scrambled, politicked, and negotiated for higher offices. Pluralistic clerics compounded the spiritual harm inflicted upon their parishes by hiring out their duties of pastoral care to inept

---

absoluciones, dispensaciones venales faciunt, quod, si aliqua beneficia sue sunt dispocioni relicta, pro questu ea conferunt, vel suis ea spuriis aut hystrionibus donant." B 2:138.76–78, 2:139.84–91 (L 1:161): "Neque enim gratiam Spiritus Sancti credendum est ab illis dari qui pecuniam propterea accipiunt, aut ab illis etiam suscipi qui tribuunt. . . . [A]utem eo est mercatore fraudulentius qui id vendit quod suum non est, quodque suo nequit emptori expedire? Quomodo autem hi nequissimi mercatores possunt diuinam gratiam tribuere, que nequaquam sui iuris est [Gratian, Decretum, C.1 q.3 c.9–11 in CIC, 1:415–17], et a qua profecto tam qui vendunt quam qui emunt alieni sunt? Quoniam, prout scriptum est: In maliuolam animam non introibit Sapientia, nec habitatit in corpore subdito peccatis: Spiritus enim Sanctus discipline effugiet fictum (Wis 1:4–5)." B 2:141.164–66 (L 1:163), following Gratian, Decretum, C.1 q.1 c.47 in CIC, 1:376–77; see also Bérier's note on this passage. Like Clamanges, Groote came close to Donatism by stating a fornicating priest was *ipso facto* excommunicated and his sacraments should be avoided. But Groote explicitly noted the efficacy of a sacrament was not voided by a suspended priest: Van Engen, "Late Medieval Anticlericalism," 29–30.

21. B 2:136.15–137.28 (L 1:160); B 2:138.80–81 (L 1:161), following Jn 17:12, 2 Thes 2:3; B 2:141.146–50 (L 1:162); B 2:147.323–25 (L 1:165).

substitutes: benefice holders often replaced themselves with uneducated mercenaries who failed in their ministry because of their ignorance and immorality.[22] Ironically, Clamanges had to explain his own holding of several benefices. In a defensive letter, he contended he earned his offices by merit, while those he charged with pluralism had gathered theirs through greed. Because he was not motivated by ambition and was content with what was necessary for living, he did not seek more benefices which, he boasted, he could have attained had he sought them.[23]

Simony was compounded when clerics sold themselves to secular bidders. These comments recall earlier complaints when Clamanges had argued against the French subtraction of obedience, criticizing clerics whose worldly ambition would lead both to their own downfall and to the erosion of ecclesiastical dignity. Shortly after the restoration of obedience, he stated those who acted this way were doomed because God would save those who put their hope in what is divine, not in what is of the flesh. Therefore, all in the Church should aim higher, aspiring to serve God before man. In an undated letter to Nicolas de Baye, Clamanges reminded his friend to store his riches in heaven and not on earth; to refrain from serving man instead of God; and to remain consistent in his service to God. He curtly told his friend he could not serve the secular world at all if he wished to serve God fully. Priests who were servants of secular princes made poor ministers, he explained in *Contra prelatos symoniacos*. They seemingly performed every common household service—including working as cooks, butlers, stewards, waiters, and storekeepers—instead of fulfilling their primary sacramental functions.[24]

---

22. B 2:140.118–25 (L 1:162); C 373.471–83 (L 2:227); B 2:134.863 (d'Achery 1:480); and especially C 370.357 (L 2:226): *"... mercenariis indoctis, ineptis, viciosis, tali ministerio indignis. ..."*

23. C 226.202–14 (L 2:138). Bernstein pointed out Clamanges was clearly guilty of pluralism and absenteeism, but he apparently did not gather offices as greedily as others since he declined a canonry on at least one occasion. He also appears to have resigned as treasurer at Langres and cantor at Bayeux as he progressed through other offices. See Bernstein, NP, 5, esp. n. 37; Alfred Coville, *Gontier et Pierre Col et l'humanisme en France au temps de Charles VI* (Paris: Droz, 1934), 85; and Ornato, *Jean Muret*, 183.

24. C 199.115–200.141 (L 2:118–19); C 593.54–594.77 (L 2:243–44), following Mt 6:20–21, Lk 12:33–34; C 598.22–599.43 (L 2:247); B 2:146.295–99 (L 1:165); C 200.155–62 (L 2:119), following Jer 17:5, Ps 52:9. Clamanges devoted the first third of *De filio prodigo*, written about this time, to declaiming in similar terms against those who, like the prodigal son,

Clamanges continued his catalogue of problems in the body of the Church by complaining repeatedly parish priests could be just as hypocritical as those above them in the hierarchy. The situation was so bad, he had written earlier in *De ruina,* that whereas previously the order of priesthood had been considered honorable and venerable, in his time nothing was seen as more abject or despicable than to be a priest.[25] He singled out for criticism the duplicity of ambitious clerics who harmed the Church, cautioning in *De studio theologico* about 1413 there was nowhere for them to hide from exposure of their hypocritical ways. Like prelates who mirrored the Pharisees of the gospels, many priests *in membris* failed to practice what they preached. Parishioners would have a difficult time following the words of these preachers who were so obviously tainted by the very matters they condemned. Clamanges repeated Jesus' admonition to His own critics: hypocritical physicians should heal themselves first and put their words into action, as He did. Clamanges even placed complaints against a hypocritical priest directly into the collective mouth of his parishioners in *De studio theologico.* The parish charged its priest with ignorance, calling him a shameless teacher *(preceptor impudicus)* who points to the east, presumably Jerusalem, but walks to the west and thereby leads the flock astray, indeed into the enemy's territory: "If you preach what is the way to Paradise, why do you not hold to that way, but proceed by its opposite?" Clamanges had the parish ask its priest. "Who would believe the words of him whom he sees to deceive by his actions? Who would have faith to follow by the way of him whom he sees to go astray?"[26]

---

endanger themselves when they seek worldly gain instead of putting their faith and efforts in divine matters. Such prodigal sons squander God's gifts, fight the Church, and tear her apart; they risk eternal penalty unless God's mercy intervenes because they crawl in the world and fail to flee to their father's house as they ought. See B 2:5.114–16 (L 1:111): *". . . in suum domicilium volare debebant et in terra repunt* (Lv 11:46): *in superna conscendere iubebantur et, nisi Deus miserando prospiciat, in inferna demerguntur* (Lk 10:15, Mt 18:6)."

25. Coville, *Le Traité,* 119: *"Olim summo in honore apud seculares sacerdocium erat et nichil venerabilius presbiterali ordine. Nunc vero nichil abjectius aut despicabilius."*

26. C 612.116–33 (L 2:152–53); B 2:112.227–37, 239–42, 244–49 (d'Achery 1:475), following Lk 4:23; B 2:113.266–71, 274–77 (d'Achery 1:475), following Jn 5:36 and 10:38, Mt 23:3; B 2:129.721–24 (d'Achery 1:479). See especially B 2:112.242–44, 249–51 (d'Achery 1:475): *"Si ea ad paradisum via est quam predicas, cur illam non tenes, sed per contrariam incedis? . . . Quis eius verbis credat quem re videt fallere? Quis fidem de via illi habeat quam videt errare?"*

To Clamanges' eyes, the most disturbing cumulative result of these problems *in membris* was the almost total lack of concern with the *cura animarum* among shepherds who were interested only in themselves. The worst pastoral difficulties within the Church, he wrote to d'Ailly, stemmed from the abundance of temporalities and luxuries, which distracted clerics from spiritual matters. Greed led to private gain, which did not serve pastoral needs. In a series of long letters to the Parisian theology student Raoul de la Porte ca. 1408–11, he attempted to remedy this situation by warning the salvation of the shepherd would be tied up with that of his sheep. Prophetic admonitions from Isaiah and Ezekiel figured prominently in these letters. Clamanges decried the fact that many watchmen who would be held accountable for their charges were in fact often blind and mute. Employing a more rhetorical style, Clamanges elaborated on this theme of blind watchmen. Who would entrust treasures to the blind?, he asked. What blind man could see an enemy coming? How could someone who was mute announce warnings against deceits and frauds? What good, after all, was a bad watchman? Such watchmen failed to see the dangers they posed to themselves and to others because they were ignorant of the knowledge and actions necessary for salvation. They did not know the way to salvation and so led their flocks astray. It was no wonder that when the blind led the blind, both fell into a pit. Clamanges ended one letter ominously by stressing that the preacher delegated by God to spread the message of salvation must not fail. Citing Daniel, Clamanges wrote that those who led many to justice would be like the eternal stars in heaven. He referred to Ezekiel, on the other hand, to warn that if the selfish preacher caring only for himself did not fulfill his task of announcing salvation and someone consequently died in sin, the sinner's blood would be on the preacher's hands. He again turned to the matter of personal responsibility, salvation, and damnation a few years later, when he repeated his admonition that every pastor would be called to account for his service: those whose poor stewardship produced ruin and calamities for the Church would find themselves doomed.[27]

27. C 177.73–83 (L 2:105); C 178.126–179.133 (L 2:106); C 358.412–17 (L 2:219); C 360.9–27 (L 2:220), following Ez 3:17–18; C 361.37–42 (L 2:220), following Is 56:10–11; C

Clamanges often underlined his calls for pastoral reform *in membris* by using the imagery of good and bad shepherds, exposed flocks, and menacing wolves. He contrasted the good shepherd with the bad in an untitled pastoral poem written very early in his career, in late September or early October 1394. This was the period between the time news of Clement VII's death reached Paris and the announcement of Benedict XIII's election followed in turn. As Dario Cecchetti has demonstrated in his study of this poem, Clamanges relied heavily on the bucolic imagery and themes of Vergil's *Georgics* in order to measure the fun-loving life of the shepherd Alexis, who neglected his flock, against the dutiful care Philarus, another shepherd, showed for his sheep. Cecchetti noted specifically that Philarus stressed the need to protect the sheep from wolves and thieves. Clamanges in this pastoral also closely paraphrased a prophecy from Ezekiel that promised a good pastor named David would restore peace and care for his flock. David would then harshly judge those shepherds who had failed to care for their sheep and instead had taken advantage of them.[28]

Clamanges used pastoral imagery throughout his career. In *De ruina*, he drew on the metaphor of shepherd and flock to charge poor shepherds with leading their flocks astray by their own bad examples. Elsewhere he adopted Christ's explanation of a bad shepherd to indict absentee pastors and the inept mercenaries they hired in their stead. Like the negligent pastors who hired them, these substitutes exposed their sheep to wolves; consequently each group was unworthy of the very name "shepherd." The iniquity of greedy clerics, he wrote more specifically in *Contra prelatos symoniacos,* led their flocks to immorality and even heresy, usually by way of their simony. The shepherds were so ignorant,

---

361.44–58 (L 2:220–21), following Mt 15:14, Lk 6:39; C 359.431–40 (L 2:219), following Dn 12:3; C 359.445–51 (L 2:219–20), following Ez 3:18–21; C 578.55–68 (L 2:326), following Lk 16:2, Is 10:3–4.

28. Cecchetti believes the prophecy of the coming good shepherd represented Clamanges' desire that a pope more concerned with the pastoral needs of Christians would succeed Clement VII, for whom he had little respect: Cecchetti, "Un'egloga inedita di Nicolas de Clamanges," in *Miscellanea di studi e ricerche sul quattrocento francese,* ed. Franco Simone (Turin: Giappichelli Editore, 1967), 25–57, especially 37–40, and Clamanges' text following Ez 34 at 54.128–57.179.

useless, and blind, with no love for their flocks at all, that Clamanges wondered in *De studio theologico* whether their presence did more harm than their absence would, reminiscent of a point Clamanges had made sarcastically over a decade earlier in *De ruina* when discussing curial prelates who were often absent from their many benefices. He again threatened such shepherds, warning that those who continued to ignore their duties of *cura animarum* would be repaid suitably.[29]

Clamanges dramatically used the image of bad shepherds in concluding *De studio theologico*. In that treatise Clamanges had Christ directly criticize His own shepherds in a prosecutorial tone, asking them why they avoided the task of shepherding; why they sought offices when they had no intention of fulfilling their tasks; why they were absent from their places of service or had put another in their stead; why they allowed wolves to attack their sheep whom they had also permitted to go hungry. Christ wondered why neglectful shepherds had no fear. How could they be ignorant of the danger to themselves if just one of their sheep were lost? Finally, Christ threatened lazy, negligent shepherds with severe penalty.[30] Clamanges went even further with his use of the imagery of wolves. Not only did negligent shepherds expose their flocks to wolves, he contended, but frequently the shepherds themselves were the wolves. They desired not the salvation of their flocks but, like wolves who preyed upon sheep, their milk and wool. This complaint was followed in Clamanges' 1414 letter to Reginald of Soissons with a reminder that, as bishop, it was up to Reginald to care for the entire flock of his diocese, parts of which were afflicted with wolves, presumably Reginald's own priests. Here Clamanges linked the reform of diocesan bishops with that of their parish priests: both should be more vigilant shepherds over their respective flocks. He reminded Reginald of Paul's order to the leaders of the

---

29. Coville, *Le Traité*, 114–15; C 367.281–84 (L 2:224); C 371.396–403 (L 2:226), following Jn 10:12–13; B 2:137.34–42, 2:138.58–63 (L 1:160–61); B 2:128.679–83, 2:128.697–129.705 (d'Achery 1:478–79).

30. B 2:129.725–130.755, 2:131.759–61 (d'Achery 1:479). Clamanges chided another correspondent to fulfill his role as shepherd or fear the consequences: C 333.49–50 (L 2:205): "*. . . alioquin, nisi hoc sedulo feceris, servi pigri et inutilis penam pertimesce. . . .*" Elsewhere he stressed that although the Lord would punish bad shepherds, as the good shepherd He would still save the sheep: C 349.55–68 (L 2:214).

community at Miletus to care for the flock entrusted to them. This point was also made to Raoul de la Porte: though pastoral care of flocks is the job of the shepherds, few performed their functions to keep their sheep as their own, be they in charge of a diocese or a parish.[31]

31. C 627.67–628.80 (L 2:343); C 628.85–91 (L 2:343), following Acts 20:28, Ez 34:2; C 371.422–372.431 (L 2:226–27). Gerson and others also wrote in such terms: Brown, *Pastor and Laity,* 48, 53, and especially 274 n. 87.

CHAPTER 5

The Reform of Scholastic Education

Clamanges' pastorally oriented views on institutional reform logically caused him to turn his attention to an aspect of reform directly related to the *reformatio in membris:* theological education that would produce well-trained, caring, and moral parish priests worthy of the title "pastor." The education of the parish priest is the crucial connection for Clamanges between personal and pastoral reform in the Church's body. Clamanges was particularly troubled by the poor quality of candidates for the priesthood and was similarly disappointed with the low examination standards of diocesan bishops who were more interested in collecting exorbitant fees for ordinations and appointments. On these points, Clamanges heralds the Council of Trent's decrees on seminaries with their emphases on personal training in heart and mind, preparation for pastoral service, and careful examination of candidates for ordination.

A step toward remedying poor pastoral situations *in membris* was to have prospective clerics concern themselves above all with preparing for the *cura animarum.* This focus was best pursued when the student worked on his own spiritual progress, another indication Clamanges did not advocate personal reform for its own sake. With the *devotio moderna,* Clamanges saw personal reform as moving outward to pastoral service: an imitation of Christ in prayer and action. Personal reform, when applied to the reform of scholastic education, would produce a pastor eager to minister worthily and charitably to his flock as he responded to the promptings of the Holy Spirit within his own heart.

This marriage of personal and pastoral reform is a major theme in Clamanges' *De studio theologico* as well as many letters on the subject in which he urged students and ministers to imitate Christ according to the examples of the disciples and Fathers. Pastors had to walk in the footsteps of Christ by following Paul and the early martyrs in giving witness to their worthiness in word and deed. Studying so they could teach, pastors should pasture their flocks instead of serving themselves, following always the good shepherd's model. More specifically, Clamanges' educational plan centered on training in Scripture and theology that was itself grounded in the grace of the Holy Spirit and dialectically related to a student's *reformatio personalis.* Such an education would instruct the *affectus* of the candidate more than fill him with idle, useless, self-serving *scientia.* As a result, the Holy Spirit would more easily direct the candidate to the proper *finis* of his studies: shepherding and preaching in charity for the salvation of those entrusted to his care.[1]

THE CONTEXT OF CRITICISM

The intellectual context at Paris was as influential on Clamanges' thought as the events of the Schism. Late medieval scholasticism was coming under increasing attack from reformers who drew on biblical, classical, and patristic models to reinvigorate education with more humanistic means and ends. They sought to apply pastoral and humanistic reform principles to a troubled university system distanced from its original purpose of training pastors for the care of souls. Much of the criticism of scholastic education in the fourteenth century centered around a style of learning that had devolved into arid speculation of theological matters that were purely academic and little more than ostentatious displays of rhetoric. Such speculative theology or *sophismata* divorced from pastoral goals grew from the medieval scholastic method that over time focused on vain questions or matters of curiosity alone.[2] Questions surrounding pastoral service and dispensations to study for the care of souls had frequently formed the topics of thirteenth-century quodlibets from Paris and Oxford. The answers of *magistri,* particularly Aquinas, were used as guides in fourteenth- and fifteenth-century manuals on education and dispensations of clerics with the *cura animarum.*

1. Among many statements of this theme see C 577.45–578.51 (L 2:326). This topic has been partially addressed by François Bérier in "La figure du clerc dans le *'De studio theologico'* de Nicolas de Clamanges," *Travaux de linguistique et de littérature* 21 (1983): 81–103.

2. Erika Rummel, *The Humanist-Scholastic Debate in the Renaissance and Reformation* (Cambridge: Harvard University Press, 1995), 1–18.

Ecclesiastical legislation also treated this topic. *Cum ex eo,* the 1298 constitution of Boniface VIII, had dealt with a number of Clamanges' later interests. *Cum ex eo* was designed to improve the education of clerics with the *cura animarum,* ironically in part by allowing their absence from benefices for study. A bishop could allow a cleric to be away from his parish for up to seven years of education, but the student had to proceed to ordination, and presumably pastoral service, within one year of finishing his studies. *Cum ex eo* also kept that student's flock in mind by making provisions for a responsible pastoral substitute during his absence. So esteemed and popular was *Cum ex eo* that it was the only dispensation permitted to continue when the delegates at Constance prohibited all others in 1418. *Cum ex eo* stood until Trent's decrees established a seminary system and prescribed a formal curriculum of studies for prospective priests.[3]

A contemporaneous example of Clamanges' criticism of theological education is offered by his close friend and frequent correspondent, Gerson. As chancellor of the University of Paris, Gerson attacked the vain and impractical curiosity of late medieval scholasticism. He complained theologians laid excessive emphasis on logic, mathematics, and scientific methods. Full of pride and arrogance, they also concerned themselves too much with excesses and innovations in terminology. Without humility, they exercised their desires to reach beyond the limits of what could be known by man. In terms Clamanges also employed, Gerson called for a return to the study of Scripture in a spirit of penitence, because when a theologian reaches beyond his limits he tries to supplant God. Gerson

---

3. Leonard E. Boyle, "The Quodlibets of St. Thomas and Pastoral Care," *The Thomist* 38 (1974): 251. Aquinas held that professional teaching was more important than pastoral service because learned scholars showed lower laborers how to do their jobs. For attempts to improve parish service in England, see Boyle, "Robert Grosseteste and the Pastoral Care," *Medieval and Renaissance Studies* 8 (1979): 3–51, especially 8–23, and "The *Oculus Sacerdotis* and Some Other Works of William of Pagula," *Transactions of the Royal Historical Society,* 5th ser., 5 (1955): 81–110. This summary follows Boyle, "The Constitution *'Cum ex eo'* of Boniface VIII," *Mediaeval Studies* 24 (1962): 263–302. The constitution was particularly aimed at improving overly strict mandates on the cleric's residency in his benefice, including *Licet canon* of Lyons II (1274), which actually prevented parochial clergy from obtaining the education necessary for the *cura animarum.* Earlier decrees, such as the 1219 statement by Honorius III incorporated into the 1234 *Decretales* as *Super specula,* had provided more for the education of professional theologians than parish priests.

stressed the need for a personal *via purgativa* and interior conversion
that would reorient theology to its proper, practical goal of pastoral service while simultaneously reminding theologians of their human limita-
tions. Gerson also emphasized an affective, mystical approach to theology that, more than intellectual exploration, would teach the truth of
Scripture through the experience of divine love.[4]

Clamanges' proposals for improving the heart and mind of the cleric
were often in agreement with the ideas of his friend Gerson, who maintained "that the whole reformation of the church rests upon the intellectual and moral conversion of its clergy." Clamanges was in line with
those of his colleagues who in committee at Constance advocated three
areas of individual clerical reform: personal morality, qualifications for
pastoral service, and pastoral care. There was concern at Constance especially that clergy charged with the care of souls be properly educated,
appropriately paid, and celibate.[5] Clamanges' goals built on the indispensable *reformatio personalis* of the candidate and continued through a
deeper appreciation of the essential role the grace of the Holy Spirit
played both in intellectual education and spiritual growth. He wished to
orient the candidate toward the proper end of study: teaching and
preaching in order to lead his flock to its salvation. This goal would be
accomplished through a solid theological education that did not devolve
into scholastic ostentation, but produced a priest who would lead the
way to God through word and deed. Like Gerson, Clamanges turned to
study as a means to this important end, seeking the personal perfection
of the cleric-in-training as a necessary prerequisite for his understanding

4. Pascoe, *Jean Gerson,* 99–109, 152–53; Steven Ozment, "The University and the
Church: Patterns of Reform in Jean Gerson," *Medievalia et Humanistica,* n.s., 1 (1970):
112–16, and *The Age of Reform 1250–1550: An Intellectual and Religious History of Late
Medieval and Reformation Europe* (New Haven: Yale University Press, 1980), 73–82. Gerson's views on education are contained principally in two lectures delivered at Paris in
November 1402, *Contra curiositatem studentium,* which may be found in Jean Gerson,
Oeuvres complètes, ed. Palémon Glorieux, 10 vols. (Paris: Desclée et Cie, 1960–73),
3:224–49. His views on a penitential theology that favored a mystical and affective
approach are contained in *De mystica theologia speculativa* (1402–3) and found in Glorieux,
3:250–92.

5. The quotation is from Pascoe, *Jean Gerson,* 124. The Constance plans for the reform
of the individual cleric were overshadowed by attempts to resolve the Schism at its highest
level: Stump, *Reforms,* 139, 149–52.

of Scripture and theology as guided by the Holy Spirit. Personal reform also prepared the scholastic for the proper exercise of his pastoral duties once he had completed his studies and passed examination. As with Gerson, for Clamanges learning became a "pastoral tool."[6] In order to understand Clamanges' conception of the reform of scholastic education, it is essential to remember that personal perfection, academic training, and pastoral activity were integrally related in his reform thought.

FAILURES OF CLERICAL TRAINING

Clamanges identified several problems with the training and performance of priests. He protested that too many candidates for the priesthood were noted for the poor quality of their education, particularly in Latin and doctrine. Priests were often unintelligent and unlearned: the worst were barely literate beyond a few words or syllables and did not even know whether they were conferring God's blessing or curse. They knew about as much Latin as they did Arabic; Clamanges complained that their Greek was so bad they could hardly distinguish an *alpha* from a *beta*. Linking poor education with intellectual confusion and immorality, Clamanges implied that because so many priests could not read well enough, they simply might not know better when it comes to their conduct. In this way, they put their flocks in danger: their poor learning offered occasion for the ambiguity, hindrance, and scandal against which Jesus and Paul had warned.[7] Unfortunately, even educated clerics cared more for the glory of learning than the pastoral service for which Clamanges believed theological training should properly prepare them.

6. The Spirit played a central role in personal reform and the cleric's education for Gerson, as well: Pascoe, *Jean Gerson,* 175–214, and Ozment, "The University and the Church," 111–26. For Gerson on preaching, see Pascoe, *Jean Gerson,* 118–28, and D. Catherine Brown, *Pastor and Laity in the Theology of Jean Gerson* (Cambridge: Cambridge University Press, 1987), 19–21, 48–55. The phrase "pastoral tool" is Mark S. Burrows', who suggests Gerson's main treatise on theology was written for clerics charged with the care of souls or perhaps for those training for this task: *Jean Gerson and De Consolatione Theologiae (1418): The Consolation of a Biblical and Reforming Theology for a Disordered Age* (Tübingen: J. C. B. Mohr [Paul Siebeck], 1991), 93, 115, 132–35.

7. B 2:146.283–87 (L 1:165); Coville, *Le Traité,* 118–19, 131. Clamanges discovered the poor quality of the Latin written and spoken at Avignon during his service there: C 96.99–101, 103–10 (L 2:58). On the links between ignorance and immorality, see Coville, *Le Traité,* 119, and C 546.759–64 (L 1:77), following Mt 18:6, Mk 9:42, Rom 14:13.

Reiterating a frequent concern, Clamanges charged these men with gathering benefices for material and personal gain instead of exercising a selfless, spiritual desire to pasture God's flock. Again utilizing vegetative imagery, Clamanges in *De studio theologico* observed that too many studied theology for the titles they could achieve rather than for the knowledge necessary for service—metaphorically, for the flower and not the fruit of study. They were more interested in obtaining a vain name and pursuing empty goals, including ostentation and ambition, than in learning sound doctrine to share with their flocks.[8]

Clamanges maintained the dangers posed by clergy who were trained poorly or whose interests lay only with themselves were compounded by an episcopal problem. The greed and ineptitude of poor candidates were rarely discovered because bishops seldom examined them properly before ordination. Episcopal examination of candidates was supposed to have been a rigid canonical mandate for the conferral of holy orders. Gratian cited the requirement of a diligent examination of candidates for priesthood from the seventh-century Council of Nantes. Under Innocent III, Lateran IV decreed in 1215 that prelates who have pastoral responsibilities should be examined for the legitimacy of their election and the worthiness of their character. They in turn were entrusted with ordaining only those candidates for priesthood who could fulfill their offices. The *Decretales* required bishops to instruct candidates properly and to refrain from ordaining any who were ignorant or unformed *(ignaros et rudes)* under threat of strict penalty. According to this conciliar legislation based on canon law and focused on pastoral care, it was better to have a few good ministers than many bad because of the gospel principle that when the blind lead the blind, both fall into a pit.[9]

The prescriptions of this legislation were sometimes tempered. The early fourteenth-century *Oculus Sacerdotis,* a guide to pastoral care writ-

8. Bérier, "La figure du clerc," 90–91; B 2:104.17–22 (d'Achery 1:473): *"Illos tantummo-do perfunctorie ac transeunter tunc meus sermo nota aliquantula perstrinxit, qui titulos magis affectant quam scientiam, florem quam frugem, nomen vanum quam dogma sanum, non ipsos quidem gradus arguens sed inanem ostentationem, sed ocium, sed inertiam, sed pompam, sed ambitionem."*

9. Nantes, c.11 as cited by Gratian, *Decretum,* Dist.24, c.5 in CIC, 1:88; Lateran IV, consts. 26–27 following X.1.14.14 in CIC, 2:130–31. The gospel reference is to Mt 15:14 and Lk 6:9.

ten by the well-educated Berkshire priest William of Pagula, advised that those to be ordained should not be held to standards that were too high. Candidates for priesthood need only be qualified, not brilliant. A bishop may even dispense with his systematic investigation into a candidate's level of understanding of the faith. According to William, "Ordinands are not to be examined too rigidly, but rather in a summary fashion, and leniently. Too great perfection is not required as long as a reasonable literacy, a legitimate age and a good character are not wanting. . . . [T]he good opinion in which a candidate is publicly held can be equivalent to an examination: indeed it is clear that local candidates of good repute are to be spared examination." [10] Lax examinations in England raised concerns because of pastoral implications. The bishop of Bath, while presiding over the first reform committee at Constance, introduced a proposal that mandated the diligent examination of ordinands on the local level. The proposal repeated the familiar charges against cursory or non-existent examinations and warned against the poor morals and education of priests that remained undiscovered as a result. Like many other reforms aimed at the Church *in membris* that were drafted in Constance's committees, however, the proposal was never legislated. A lax *examinatio* was common enough almost one hundred and fifty years later that the Council of Trent in its *Decreta super reformatione* reasserted Gratian's use of the Council of Nantes' decree. Trent mandated a bishop must diligently investigate and examine a candidate's "family, personality, age, education, conduct, doctrine and faith." [11]

The lack of an *examinatio* that so concerned canon lawyers and council delegates was also very troubling for Clamanges. He held the poor *examinatio* was itself a natural consequence of simony that frequently resulted in the appointment of a priest untrained for pastoral service. The candidate did not worry about his eloquence, training, or the merits of his life, only that he had enough money to purchase the office he

10. Boyle, "The *Oculus Sacerdotis*," 92. Brown believes Gerson would have agreed with William's statement, which she cites: *Pastor and Laity*, 50. William J. Dohar describes ordination scrutinies in *"Sufficienter litteratus*: Clerical Examination and Instruction for the Cure of Souls," in *A Distinct Voice: Medieval Studies in Honor of Leonard E. Boyle, O.P.*, ed. Jacqueline Brown and William P. Stoneman (Notre Dame: University of Notre Dame Press, 1997), 305–21.

11. Stump, *Reforms*, 150, with the text of the proposal at 375–76; Trent, session 23, c.7.

sought. Because local bishops cared not for the quality of the candidates who came before them but only for their own purses, they quickly ordained to the priesthood almost anyone proposed. There was often no episcopal *examinatio* at all; consequently many candidates who did not even know the basics of Latin were ordained and secured appointments. Clamanges regretted the frequent result: an unexamined, unqualified, and immoral pastor placed before a parish.[12]

THE IDEAL CANDIDATE: PERSONALLY REFORMED, PASTORALLY ORIENTED

Clamanges regarded the offices of pastor and doctor as essentially identical, following the Pauline delineation. Equating office with function, Clamanges described the theology doctor/pastor as a worthy minister who should shepherd and teach. He held that the theologian should always keep in mind his primary goal of teaching, comparing him to a ministering angel sent by God to announce divine laws. This mission should not be taken for granted: although the cloak and biretta of the doctor should be an outer sign of his inner worth, they did not necessarily make him a worthy teacher. That distinction must be earned and not assumed by the mere attainment of a theology doctorate.[13] Clamanges discussed several of the ideal theologian's central tasks, beginning with the obligation to preach frequently and diligently. This task was informed by Clamanges' adoption of the role of the classical orator. Emulating the classical model, the humanist was originally and foremost

12. B 2:140.134–38 (L 1:162); B 2:145.278–146.281 (L 1:164–65); Coville, *Le Traité*, 115; B 2:136.9–10 (L 1:160); B 2:147.309–12 (L 1:165). Gerson assigned the primary responsibility of finding worthy candidates to the bishop, a duty that conformed to his emphasis on episcopal leadership in reform. According to Gerson, the candidate suitable for pastoral service should be eloquent, persuasive, and contemplative; should have a solid understanding of Scripture, theology, and morality; and should lead his flock by his own example of good deeds. The better educated the candidate, as determined by a good examination, the better he would preach: Pascoe, *Jean Gerson*, 120–25, 170–71.

13. Bérier, "La figure du clerc," 88. B 2:105.32–54 (d'Achery 1:473), especially 35–38 and 39–42 expounding on Eph 4:11 and 1 Cor 12:28: *"Et vide quod duo nouissima* [pastors and doctors] *signanter inuicem coniunxit, cum superiora singula possuisset, vt intelligant qui pastores sunt doctores se esse debere. . . . Non sunt ergo pastores nisi qui doctores, nec doctores vicissim habendi nisi iidem pastores sint. Ad quid autem instituti sunt in Christi Ecclesia pastores et doctores nisi ad pascendum et docendum?"* See also C 199.96–101 (L 2:118); C 367.284–87 (L 2:224); B 2:108.120–24 (d'Achery 1:474); B 2:133.829–30 (d'Achery 1:480).

a professional teacher—an active *rhetor*. With the movement away from the arid excesses of scholasticism in which Clamanges and Gerson participated, a *theologia rhetorica* developed that married classical ideals of eloquence with clear points of theology. The preacher was to make theology intelligible for his broad audience. While the model for the classical orator was of course Cicero, Clamanges and other late medieval humanists turned also to late antique Christian examples, especially Jerome, Augustine, and Basil the Great. Among the Fathers they found models of moral, eloquent, and learned preachers who did not befuddle their audiences, but illuminated and edified them with the message of Scripture.[14]

Clamanges stressed the importance of this type of learned preacher in the Fathers' image. Because the preacher is called, preaching is a vocation: like the prophets, the preacher is anointed and receives a revelation he is bound to share. Clamanges in this context again focused on the dialectical relationship between personal reform and pastoral service. In addition to his words, the preacher must lead by example to bring others to God as Christ did. It was more important, Clamanges advised, to provide a good example by living well than by speaking neatly.[15] Clamanges here joined Gerson and other reforming preachers of the era, including Vincent Ferrer and Bernardino of Siena, in maintaining that the light of a preacher's inner life should shine outward as an example for others to follow. These positive exhortations were complemented by practical con-

14. Bérier, "La figure du clerc," 93–102. Bérier notes Clamanges' concern with the preacher's religious tasks of providing a good example, shepherding his flock, teaching for salvation, and preaching to prevent heresy. But he is more concerned with Clamanges' depiction of the ideal preacher as the late medieval heir of the honorable, eloquent public servant in the classical mode. For discussions of Clamanges' interest in Ciceronian rhetoric, see Cecchetti, "'*Sic me Cicero laudare docuerat.*' La retorica nel primo umanesimo francese," in *Préludes à la Renaissance. Aspects de la vie intellectuelle en France au XVe siècle,* ed. Carla Bozzolo and Ezio Ornato (Paris: Éditions du CNRS, 1992), 47–106, and *Petrarca, Pietramala e Clamanges. Storia di una "querelle" inventata* (Paris: Éditions CEMI, 1982), 205–25. On the Fathers as late medieval models, see also John F. D'Amico, "Humanism and Pre-Reformation Theology," in *Renaissance Humanism: Foundations, Forms, and Legacy,* 3 vols., ed. Albert Rabil, Jr. (Philadelphia: University of Pennsylvania Press, 1988), 3:355–57. E. F. Jacob noted as an example Clamanges' gratitude to Gontier Col for sending him a volume of Jerome and Augustine's writings: "Christian Humanism," in *Europe in the Late Middle Ages,* ed. J. R. Hale et al. (Evanston, Ill.: Northwestern University Press, 1965), 448–50.

15. C 366.244–47 (L 2:224), following Rom 10:15, Heb 5:4; C 368.311–14 (L 2:225); B 2:111.212–14 (d'Achery 1:474); B 2:127.652–55 (d'Achery 1:478); C 467.192–94 (L 2:278–79).

cerns and negative prodding. The preacher would be more credible to
his listeners if he heeded his own reproaches. He should move his listeners more by his good deeds and moral examples than by his words; otherwise, he could be charged with the very faults he chastised. Clamanges
also warned the negligent preacher by citing the Letter of James: whoever knows what is good but does not do it is sinful.[16]

How the prospective pastor learned what was good and how to act,
minister, and preach accordingly was a function of his own personal perfection through study. The Holy Spirit is the vivifying element in this
intellectual and affective education of the prospective pastor. The Holy
Spirit, according to Clamanges, would enlighten the scholastic's heart,
producing in him an inflamed *affectus* through prayer and meditation.
The Holy Spirit would also help him to understand through study the
content *(scientia)* of the faith that he would be preaching. *Affectus* and
scientia were both integrated and discrete components of the student's
education. Priority was to be given to the lessons of meditation and
prayer that infused the student's *affectus* and informed his charitable pastoral service. Meditation through the grace of the Holy Spirit leads to
the growth of charity within the heart of the cleric. This charity is then
communicated to his listeners.[17] Study, intellectual enlightenment, and
scientia, however, were not overlooked but clarified by Clamanges, who
placed them within the context of the *affectus.* True knowledge touches
hearts and minds: it instructs the intellect as it infuses the *affectus* for the
progress of the pastor and his flock. The grace of the Holy Spirit thus

16. B 2:122.504–14 (d'Achery 1:477); C 346.246–347.254 (L 2:212–13), especially 252–54:
*"Ita enim debet vivere conversarique predicator, ut plus opere et exemplo quam sermone et elo-
quio suos m[o]veat auditores."* C 366.231–32 (L 2:223), following Jas 4:17. On the similar
message of Gerson and other contemporaries, see Brown, *Pastor and Laity,* 20–21, 49,
52–55.

17. Bérier, "La figure du clerc," 89–90. The rest of the paragraph that Bérier cited
makes even clearer the connection between the pure heart of the cleric and his mission of
pastoral ministry, a reminder that the ultimate goal of Clamanges' program of a reformed
clerical education was the conversion of parishioners: B 2:116.358–117.367 (d'Achery 1:476):
*"Illa etenim Lex sancta et spiritualis et immaculata convertens animas, si attenta investigatione
ac meditatione ruminetur, munda animalia facit et digna Domino offerri; spirituales in
hominibus maxime parit affectus, vtpote a Spiritu Sancto instituta.*

*Hos autem inducendo carnales educit, mundanos expellit, vagos et curiosos exturbat.
Gaudet admodum Spiritus Sanctus dum ex ore predicatoris sua audit verba sonare; illis adest,
illa dirigit, illa sequitur et comitatur, et in cordibus impressa audientium fructificare facit."*

fills the heart of those studying properly and reveals to them the profound mysteries of the faith. Without this revelation by the grace of the Holy Spirit, no one could know the depths of God or make that knowledge known to others.[18]

Clamanges once again gathered together personal reform, clerical education, and pastoral service when he enjoined the theology student to study diligently, but to aim for tasks and rewards higher than what the academic or material world offered. Spiritual rewards were found in the lessons of Scripture, which taught pastors and Christians all they needed to know. Clamanges pointed this out in *De prosperitate aduersitatis* when explaining the consolation of Scripture as an essential component of the *reformatio personalis*. He commended the study of Scripture to Nicolas de Baye, telling him that by studying Scripture he would with God's grace learn the precious value of eloquence, clear judgment, wisdom, and virtue.

But academic accomplishment should not make a student feel he was better than his charges, Clamanges wrote in *De studio theologico*. As a scholastic's learning increased, so should his humility rise. Clamanges was especially concerned in *De studio theologico* and his letters with students who acquired knowledge for its own sake. They became arrogant and failed to act charitably. He therefore circumscribed *scientia*, which served no pastoral end: *scientia* without *caritas* would not lead to salvation because it was not aimed at the proper end of preaching. "Knowledge inflates," he wrote, citing 1 Cor 8:1, but "love builds up." Love was the lamp's oil that, shining from within the heart of the personally reformed cleric, could not run out. Study that did not include charity was simply *curiositas;* neither correction nor anything good at all could be accomplished without *caritas*.[19]

18. B 2:120.461–65 (d'Achery 1:476–77): *"Illa est vera scientia que theologum decet, quamque omnis debet theologus expetere, que non modo intellectum instruat sed infundat simul atque imbuat affectum. Per hanc et sibi homo proficit et aliis; per hanc placere Deo in primis studet et illud opere exequi."* See also B 2:117.379–89 (d'Achery 1:476), following 1 Cor 2:10–11.

19. C 198.72–84 (L 2:118); C 199.115–200.141 (L 2:118–19); C 401.58–62 (L 2:237); B 2:124.562–64 (d'Achery 1:477); B 2:127.663–64 (d'Achery 1:478); B 2:123.540–41 (d'Achery 1:477); C 356.332–33 (L 2:218); C 577.40–45 (L 2:325–26); B 2:121.490–122.509 (d'Achery 1:477), extrapolating from the parable of the kingdom of heaven in which ten wise and

The proper *finis* of study for Clamanges was loving service in preaching that led others *ad salutem eternam,* a phrase that along with *ad vitam
eternam* occurred frequently throughout *De studio theologico.*[20] This goal
was why the cleric studied and was also the standard by which his ministry would be measured. The pastor should follow the examples of
Christ, the disciples, and the Fathers, who studied not for themselves
but to teach others. He who held the office of teacher but cared not for
the salvation of his brother, by contrast, simply could not be said to love
God. The preacher was especially charged by Clamanges with the task of
recalling sinners to God, once again following Christ's example. The
preacher gave his flock what they needed to be good Christians, ready
for their day of judgment, by providing them with knowledge of God
drawn from Scripture and the Fathers.[21]

The preacher accomplished this pastoral goal of leading others to salvation through his own *reformatio personalis,* his enlightened *affectus,*
and his education in the faith. Again, the Holy Spirit bound these elements together because the heart of the preacher could only ascend by
its fire. With Augustine in his commentary on Ps 103:4, Clamanges held

---

foolish virgins greet the bridegroom (Mt 25:1–13). Gerson also cited 1 Cor 8:1 to admonish
theologians with no concern for their parishioners: Burrows, *Jean Gerson and De Consolatione Theologiae,* 221–22.

20. Bérier, "La figure du clerc," 90–92, 96. In addition to the passages cited by Bérier,
see two parallels: B 2:123.551–54 (d'Achery 1:477) and B 2:125.599–605 (d'Achery 1:478).

21. C 577.45–578.51 (L 2:326), following Mt 28:19; B 2:119.427–29, 434–44 (d'Achery
1:476), following Jn 15:15; and especially B 2:120.475–121.485 (d'Achery 1:477): *"Isti sunt
fines quorum gratia omnis debet theologus studere, et ad quos suum totum conferre studium, in
his assidue versari, iugiter exerceri, quoniam in his tota Legis pendet perfectio totaque summa
Scripturarum, immo vite humane, ad hec referenda est. Plenitudo namque Legis, sicut apostolica nos docet auctoritas, est dilectio* (Rom 13:10). *Quomodo autem diligit Deum, qui fratris
salutem negligit? Qui non diligit fratrem suum, quem videt, Deum, quem non videt, quomodo
potest diligere? Verba sunt Beati Iohannis in epistola* (1 Jn 4:20). *Quomodo autem fratrem
diligit qui illius pro viribus saluti subuenire non curat, maxime si artem docendi habet,
locumque et officium tenet?"* Clamanges gathered many of his themes and images about the
pastoral role of the preacher in one of his long letters to Raoul de la Porte: C 365.210–18 (L
2:223): *"Quo de genere illi nimirum sunt, qui sacrarum scripturarum celesti speculationi salu-
tarique intelligentie vigilanter incumbunt, studentque de fonte illo limpidissimo aquam vivam
haurire sitientibusque refundere. Hi autem, etsi speculatores propter illius vere speculative doctrine studium atque exercitium iure vocantur, canes etiam tamen a latratu predicationis, quo
lupos terrent et effugant gregemque servant ac instruunt et, ut sibi ab eorum insidiis caveant,
admonent, merito dici possunt."*

that only when a preacher's own heart was inflamed by the Holy Spirit could his words in turn penetrate and inflame the hearts of his listeners. Clamanges here built on Augustine with his own combination of personal reform, an inflamed *affectus,* committed pastoral service, and deep learning. Augustine emphasized in *De doctrina Christiana* that the preacher must possess wisdom and internal knowledge of divine matters through the study of Scripture; only then could he relate theological topics credibly and eloquently to his listeners. Clamanges also relied on the marriage of eloquence and wisdom, repeatedly advising that the true preacher must speak to the souls of his listeners, not just to their minds. The preacher should set hearts on fire through warnings, allurements, enticements, and promises. But more than provide talk, the preacher must take action and exercise his ministry in order to help people turn away from sin and vice.[22]

For Clamanges, the ideal theology doctor trained by the Holy Spirit in heart and mind would also be a pastor ready to work in the field, instead of simply disputing academic questions or talking about working. His pragmatic concern with this *finis* of study is illustrated throughout *De studio theologico* as well as the many letters of encouragement and advice he sent to younger friends in which—as he did with respect to Reginald, the bishop of Soissons—Clamanges adopted the persona of Paul sending Timothy off on mission. Writing to Raoul de la Porte, Clamanges reminded the young theology bachelor that as a preacher he must get to work like the good and faithful servant: he must fulfill his task of drawing the faithful to a life of virtue and usefulness, while deterring them from poison and the vices. In another letter Clamanges told

---

22. C 334.95–100 (L 2:206); C 340.14–30 (L 2:209); C 351.146–48 (L 2:215); and especially B 2:114.281–82, 284–87 (d'Achery 1:475): *"Quomodo corda accendet qui sine igne est? . . . Virtutem voci predicatoris spiritus Sanctus tribuit, cor eius zelo caritatis inflammans. Illa est que cordo penetrat et transfigit intimisque facit herere verba precordiis . . ."* For the Augustinian precedent, see his sermon 2.4 on Ps 103 in *Enarrationes in Psalmos,* CC 40:1493: *"Nisi enim ardeat minister praedicans, non accendit eum cui praedicat."* On Clamanges' treatment of the relationship between eloquence and wisdom from Ciceronian and Augustinian sources, see Cecchetti, *"'Sic me Cicero laudare docuerat,'"* 50, 58–59, 84–86, and Bérier, "La figure du clerc," 99–103. Jerrold E. Siegel offers a complete discussion in *Rhetoric and Philosophy in Renaissance Humanism. The Union of Eloquence and Wisdom: Petrarch to Valla* (Princeton: Princeton University Press, 1968).

de la Porte that, like Christ raising Lazarus from the dead, the preacher must recall Christians from the sepulchre of the pattern of their sins. He must gently free captives from their sin and return exiles to the right and certain way.[23]

Clamanges used two other images to inspire the personally reformed and pastorally oriented preacher in his work. The first image was that of a mirror. The preacher must show blind sinners the errors of their ways as if holding a mirror to a woman who did not otherwise see blemishes on her face. Once she saw them, she rushed to their attention.[24] The second image, which occurred more frequently, was that the preacher was like a medical doctor. With this imagery, he tapped into a fundamental medieval identification of physical sickness with sin that itself relied on a patristic tradition we have already encountered in Clamanges' writings. Building on the Fathers, Bonaventure in his *Breviloquium* had discussed Christ as a physician offering the sacraments as spiritual medicine. Closer to Clamanges' own era, the Carthusian Ludolf of Saxony also presented Christ as a doctor in *De vita Christiana*.[25] Clamanges similarly described the preacher as a spiritual doctor and solid preaching as preventive medicine. While doctors are necessary, it is better to be in good health than to require a doctor when there is plague or fever. Like the medical doctor who should be out visiting and mending the sick rather than discussing such matters in school without ever experiencing death

23. B 2:132.794–95 (d'Achery 1:479); B 2:135.872–78 (d'Achery 1:480); C 331.9–332.18 (L 2:204), following Mt 25:14–28, Lk 19:12–24; C 341.33–45 (L 2:209); C 341.50–58 (L 2:210), following Jn 11:39. See especially the direct commands to de la Porte—like those he boldly issued to Benedict XIII and Reginald of Soissons—at C 332.34–333.45 (L 2:205): *"Age ergo, iam seculi liber compedibus, tuum laborem aggredere, tuum cursum alacriter confice, ad tuum exequendum officium studiose ac vigilanter accinge, Predica verbum, insta oportune, importune (2 Tm 4:2), ad virtutes corda fidelium ignito Dei eloquio accede, a viciis deterre, bona doce, mala dedoce, utilia semina, noxia evelle, argue obsecra, increpa in omni patientia et doctrina (2 Tm 4:2), opus fac evangeliste, ministerium tuum imple (2 Tm 4:5), ei qui te rebus ditavit, verbis saltem vicem repende gratiotum."*

24. C 372.455–63 (L 2:227).

25. Darrel W. Amundsen, "The Medieval Catholic Tradition," in *Caring and Curing: Health and Medicine in the Western Religious Traditions*, ed. Ronald L. Numbers and Darrel W. Amundsen (New York: Macmillan, 1986), 65–107, and *Dictionnaire de spiritualité ascétique et mystique doctrine et histoire*, 10:891–901, s.v. "médecin (le Christ)," by Gervais Dumeige. The passage in Bonaventure's *Breviloquium* is from part 6 as found in *Opera Omnia*, 5:265–80 (Quaracchi: Collegium S. Bonaventurae, 1891); Ludolf's treatment is in *De vita Christiana*, I.22.4 and 31.5.

or wounds, the theology doctor should preach and minister rather than just talk about these pastoral tasks. Clamanges recalled Christ's remark that He came because the sick needed a physician, not the healthy, and to recall to repentance not the just but sinners.[26]

Finally, like many contemporary reformers Clamanges criticized impractical sophistry that was divorced from personal and pastoral concerns. *Devotio moderna* followers also opposed theological education that benefitted only the scholar; the whole point of studying theology was to improve one's own spiritual life and to serve others on their journeys to God. According to Florens Radewijns (an early companion of Geert Groote) and Thomas à Kempis, it was better to live with God's grace and to experience divine love than to attain precise but self-serving book knowledge of God that served no interior devotional purpose. In line with these complaints, Clamanges lamented that theologians did not refrain from disputing topics involving sterile theological subtleties that had nothing to do with pastoral matters. Like Gerson, who as chancellor at Paris brought the Dominicans back to teach effective preaching in 1403, Clamanges held that preachers should speak usefully, not subtly. He saw too few preachers spreading their learning to practical use. In a letter addressed to Parisian scholastics, Clamanges complained their quibbling often led to quarreling under the guise of clarifying theological matters; he advised them there was no honor in this exercise. Steven Ozment asserted that with these complaints Clamanges exhibited "strong anti-intellectual tendencies." But the entirety of Clamanges' *De studio theologico* and his many letters exhorting friends to diligent study attest that he was not anti-intellectual. Like members of the *devotio moderna* Clamanges did, however, stand against the kind of intellectualism to which many humanists objected. With them, Clamanges unswervingly pointed theology students to their goal of pastoral service, as Ozment noted.[27]

26. Bérier, "La figure du clerc," 91; B 2:132.789–91, 800–805 (d'Achery 1:479); C 347.13–15 (L 2:213), following Mt 9:12–13, Mk 2:17, Lk 5:31–32; C 351.145–46 (L 2:215).

27. B 2:118.403–8 (d'Achery 1:476), following 1 Tm 6:4; B 2:120.457–60 (d'Achery 1:476); B 2.122.531–123.532 (d'Achery 1:477); C 527.58–65 (L 1:66). Petrarch also complained that scholastic theologians often argued with no practical purpose: D'Amico, "Humanism and Pre-Reformation Theology," 3:352. See also Ozment, *The Age of Reform,*

Clamanges related the reform of scholastic education to the dialectical relationship among personal reform, pastoral service, and preaching
in his letter to a theology bachelor. After congratulating him on his
study of preaching, Clamanges exhorted the young student to continue
to learn how to flood his listeners with God's living waters of salvation.
Clamanges quickly reminded the student not to study for vain curiosity
or worldly praise, but to allow himself to be inspired by the Holy Spirit.
He specifically warned against empty knowledge born from ambition
and the desire for material gain that produced nothing. Clamanges
encouraged him to pursue inner goodness that would radiate out and act
as a beacon for his flock. He repeated his caveat of a grave danger: some
students progress in academic knowledge and degrees while failing to
advance themselves or others in virtue toward God and salvation. Clamanges in this letter returned to vegetative imagery and the theme of the
relative merits of divine aid and human action in reform. He noted that
although only God could ultimately give the increase to one who plants
and waters, men must still take action with divine assistance to produce
a healthy harvest. Because of this promised aid, a pastor should not
allow his heart to grow tepid: he must work in God's garden to harvest
fruit and to inflame the hearts of his flock with light. He defined the
tasks of the true theologian as increasing truth, knowledge, and wisdom
of divine matters; as living well; and as teaching correctly not so much
through books as through hearts. Clamanges used Paul's words to Timothy to make his point that the pastor must labor as a good soldier of
Christ: preaching, acting, convincing, rebuking, staying vigilant, ministering. He sealed his exhortation with the promise that if his young
friend succeeded in performing these tasks, he would earn the title of the
good and faithful servant.[28]

78–80; and John Van Engen, "Late Medieval Anticlericalism: The Case of the New
Devout," in *Anticlericalism in Late Medieval and Early Modern Europe,* ed. Peter A. Dykema and Heiko A. Oberman (Leiden: E. J. Brill, 1993), 46–48.
    28. C 299.3–10, 17–28 (L 2:184), following Nm 20:6, Jer 2:13, Is 12:3, Sir 33:18, 1 Cor 8:1;
C 301.89–302.102 (L 2:186); C 302.121–303.141 (L 2:186), following 1 Cor 3:7, Jn 15:5, Eccl
9:10 and 11:6, 2 Tm 2:3 and 4:2, 5. Clamanges turned to the parable of the talents with its
image of the good and faithful servant three times in another letter: C 299.10–16 (L
2:184–85), C 300.45–54 (L 2:185), and C 303.146–54 (L 2:186–87), following Mt 25:14–28,
Lk 19:12–24.

CHAPTER 6

Clamanges' Place in the History of Reform

The central aspect of Clamanges' reform thought is *reformatio personalis:* it was his *sine qua non* for late medieval Church reform. That personal reform was essentially a *via purgativa* which attempted to imitate the life and works of Christ within the context of the mainstream devotions of the late Middle Ages. Clamanges' normative emphasis on personal reform was not completely divorced from the position of contemporary reformers such as Gerson. But Gerson located personal reform in a different position within a hierarchical framework: personal reform was a product of hierarchical reform in Gerson's top-down program intended to touch every part of the Church.[1] Clamanges placed personal reform first. His ideas, however, did not simply invert the top-down thinking of Gerson and most other Constance reformers. Clamanges positioned personal reform in a central location. His was an inside-out reform that radiated from the heart of the individual Christian through the rest of the Church. Keys to personal reform were fear and humility, which were themselves deeply patristic and monastic in origin, especially as they were applied to the desire for the solitude and asceticism that nurtured personal spiritual growth. Moreover, we see in Clamanges' writings the influence of the major humanistic and spiritual movements of the late Middle Ages. In their critiques of the prevailing scholastic methods, humanists adapted patristic and monastic traditions of contemplation and learning to stimulate reform during turbulent times for the institutional Church.

Personal reform for Clamanges was never an end in itself. He always

---

1. Pascoe, *Jean Gerson*, 211.

kept foremost in his writings the pastoral role of the clergy throughout the ecclesiastical hierarchy. All of the problems of simony, hypocrisy, and immorality must be overcome so the spiritual care of the Christian would be met by worthy, faithful, and exemplary pastors. These goals were particularly evident in Clamanges' recommendations concerning the reform of the Church *in membris*. Personal and pastoral reform were closely linked in Clamanges' mind, as they would be at Trent. The entire reform of clerical education was focused on the personal reform of the cleric-in-training so the ordained pastor would be a credible example to his flock. In order for this goal to be met, the theology student had to sustain a continual *reformatio personalis* under the Holy Spirit's guidance. The Holy Spirit would not only guide his personal reform, but also inflame his heart and open his mind to the lessons of Scripture. Only when this inner reform had occurred could the student effectively minister to a flock and kindle in the hearts of others the same fire that burned within his own.

These ideas of personal reform in Clamanges' thought were patristic, specifically Pauline and Augustinian. He followed Paul's emphasis on sanctification as a continual process by a Christian acting with the Holy Spirit's aid. Like Augustine in *De doctrina Christiana,* Clamanges identified several central elements of personal reform: penance, continual conversion, and learning. With Augustine and in distinction to the eastern Fathers, Clamanges linked the *vita contemplativa* with the *vita activa* to portray personal reform as a *vita mixta*. Clamanges agreed with Augustine that outward movement was the natural result of personal reform. Once a Christian had learned and was living the faith, he could not have anything but a charitable response: teaching the faith by word and deed to fellow pilgrims on the spiritual journey.[2]

In an attempt to practice what he preached concerning the urgent need for reform and the human ability to effect these necessary changes, Clamanges took up the task of the reformer. We may ask if Clamanges acted out of a genuine and selfless desire to help others or, motivated by sincerity but also self-preservation, he carefully chose to participate in

2. Ladner, *The Idea of Reform,* 334–40, 373–77.

reform efforts from afar while deliberately insulating his career from damage.[3]

Clamanges never lost interest in the great questions of reform. But he involved himself in these matters through his writings and was often absent from the inner circles of power.[4] He largely exercised his self-defined role as a reformer behind the scenes and worked from exile. Clamanges attempted to do what apparently he thought he did best: offer the fruits of his life of contemplation to those such as d'Ailly and Gerson whose personal characteristics and political connections put them in a more practical position to reform the late medieval Church. We have already heard Clamanges identify himself as a good servant in his interpretation of the parable of the talents. As university *rédacteur* and papal secretary, Clamanges was openly involved in the great affairs of 1394 to 1398. He objected to the withdrawal of obedience and through his letters he actively worked for the restoration of obedience—albeit from the relative safety of Langres—and then in 1403 he returned to papal service for five years. The consequences of his activities in the middle of this debate and others conspired to install him more permanently in his preferred role of a reformer behind the scenes. There he could protect himself from the politicking that was so damaging to his personal life and professional career. He enjoyed a fruitful active exile from 1398 to 1403 and, after 1408, engaged in a second and longer active exile until his return to the Collège de Navarre. This preference, in turn, led him to take up more programmatically a spiritual approach to personal and pastoral reform. Evidence comes from a letter Clamanges attached to a copy of *De fructu heremi* he sent to d'Ailly in 1412. Clamanges told d'Ailly that since passing leisure with no activity led to vice, he devoted his quiet time at Fontaine-au-Bois to spiritually-edifying consideration of important themes, such as the fruits of the eremitical life.[5]

3. Ornato doubts the sincerity of Clamanges' stated preference for the solitary life and sees it as a cover for his real motivation, which Ornato identifies as self-interest: *Jean Muret*, 67–81; see also B 1:xlii–xliii, lii.

4. Bernstein advanced the idea that Clamanges "did not deny himself all avenues to influence": NP, 7, 10, 16–20.

5. B 2:appendix II.

It is possible, on the other hand, to see Clamanges intentionally hiding from taking responsibility for his actions, as well as trying to insure for himself the most personally advantageous situations in his active exiles. He seems to have had something of a love-hate relationship with the center of power: wanting to be involved, but taking steps to avoid danger. There are indications of a tendency toward self-preservation. He did, after all, write to both Charles VI and Benedict XIII at a time when the Valois family and the Avignon curia increasingly opposed each other, an action that indicates his attempt to play both sides. He clearly wanted to be noticed and involved in affairs—but from a safe distance: thus his barrage of letters and the copy of his collected works that he sent to Alfonso V of Aragon. He also wrote to Henry V of England and Philip the Good in hopes of gaining their protection.

The evidence pointing toward self-preservation is not entirely damning when taken in context, however. Many royal, papal, and academic clients frequently balanced service to multiple patrons with competing loyalties at a time of shifting alliances. Even opponents such as d'Ailly, who fought the French withdrawal of obedience, and its champion Simon de Cramaud cultivated a variety of benefactors during this period. What can be viewed as shameless, politically-motivated self-preservation can also be interpreted as shrewd negotiation.[6] The challenge for many, including Clamanges, was to remain involved while avoiding entanglements that would destroy a career and banish one from any participation in the key issues of reform and the Schism. Viewed in this light, Clamanges' preference for his self-defined role behind the scenes can be, at the same time, an exercise in self-preservation and a sincere attempt to contribute to Church reform in a manner that fit both his circumstances during unprecedented tumult and his personality—which may fairly be described as cagey or waffling. Clamanges' writings, especially his many letters, can be seen as a coward's attempt to be relevant from a safe distance or as a clever way to enter the debates without getting swamped by the whirlpool of negotiations. Both assessments

---

6. Case studies are in Christopher M. Bellitto, "The Early Development of Pierre d'Ailly's Conciliarism," *Catholic Historical Review* 83 (1997): 217–32, and Howard Kaminsky, "The Early Career of Simon de Cramaud," *Speculum* 49 (1974): 499–534.

may be simultaneously accurate. Though Clamanges was clearly a selfish player, it remains true that he did contribute to the debates of his day.

The best way at getting at Clamanges the man is to see him in comparison with d'Ailly and especially Gerson, with whom he shared a close friendship from the time they met at the Collège de Navarre. With d'Ailly, Gerson focused on the details of resolving the Schism and justifying conciliar authority in the years leading up to and including Constance, but Clamanges held back and considered the questions of the late medieval Church from the relative quiet of his retreats. Possibly because he was not personally disposed to withstanding the vicissitudes of ecclesiastical politics, Clamanges protected himself. Far from the tumult and political turmoil of Paris and Constance, Clamanges was able to make bolder statements and proposals than his friends d'Ailly and Gerson, who were delicately negotiating the minefields inherent in their roles as University of Paris chancellors, theologians, and leaders at Constance. While they were resolving the Schism, Clamanges quite literally had the luxury to take a broader view of the reform of the *Ecclesia*. As Clamanges admitted, Gerson's high profile disposition, skill, and circumstances contributed to the fact that, like d'Ailly and in contrast to Clamanges, Gerson took up his role as a church statesman focused on the uppermost levels of the ecclesiastical hierarchy. Clamanges, meanwhile, complemented his friends by concerning himself primarily with reform *in membris*. Although Gerson had great personal interest in the lower levels of the hierarchy and concerned himself with improving the condition of the exercise of the faith *in membris* as often as he could, he did not have the opportunity that Clamanges embraced to devote his full attention to the Church's body until late in his career.[7] Clamanges was also more vociferous and less circumspect than Gerson, especially in letters to friends, Charles VI, and Benedict XIII. Since Clamanges was away in his retreats, he could afford to be bolder than Gerson, who demonstrated a certain "irenicism" in his writings because of his delicate positions at Paris and Constance.[8] It is interesting to note, however, that

---

7. Pascoe, *Jean Gerson*, 210, and D. Catherine Brown, *Pastor and Laity in the Theology of Jean Gerson* (Cambridge: Cambridge University Press, 1987), passim.

8. The word is Pascoe's in *Jean Gerson*, 213.

some of Clamanges' most forward and starkest comments on the state of
the late medieval Church came not from the period of his second active
exile but during the earlier part of his public career when he was more
subject to criticism and censure. In his statements urging the king, the
pope, and his friends to take up the cause of reform, as well as in his
amicable criticisms of Gerson's patience, Clamanges seems to have been
a more outspoken, restless, and even angrier reformer than his friends.

We identify Clamanges as a religious figure whose writings allow us
to add further details to the portrait of late medieval Christianity as a
vibrant and vital era of faith and devotion despite the Church's admitted
moral decadence and institutional chaos. Even the era's arithmetical
piety and loud criticisms of the clergy offer evidence of a spiritual yearn-
ing and an upsurge in religious sentiment. Clamanges' ideas belong to
that body of Catholic reform writings offered before the Protestant
Reformation that allow us to reconsider and to revise charges made
against the Catholic Church in that era and afterwards that she was
completely blind to her own faults and was, in essence, rescued by
Protestant criticisms.[9] The *devotio moderna* has already been seen as an
example of interiority and spiritual reform during the Schism. Observant orders offer similar evidence, as Kaspar Elm demonstrated. For
Elm, late medieval observant orders indicate decline and crisis on the
one hand, and restoration and revitalization on the other. Calls for
reform among religious orders indicate a perceived need for reform and
a plan of correction.[10]

Clamanges' writings demonstrate that, despite the Avignon papacy
and the Great Schism, the spirit of reform persisted in the late Middle
Ages, especially as that reform was focused not on the highest echelons
of power politics but on individual Christians. Personal reform such as
that advocated and exercised by Clamanges endured in the face of insti-

9. This reappraisal of Catholic reform has been argued by, among others, Francis Oak-
ley, *The Western Church in the Later Middle Ages* (Ithaca: Cornell University Press, 1979);
John C. Olin, ed., *Catholic Reform: From Cardinal Ximenes to the Council of Trent 1495–1563*
(New York: Fordham University Press, 1990); and H. O. Evennett, *The Spirit of the
Counter-Reformation* (Cambridge: Cambridge University Press, 1968).

10. Kaspar Elm, "Reform- und Observanzbestrebungen im Spätmittelalterlichen
Ordenswesen. Ein Überblick," in *Reformbemühungen und Observanzbestrebungen im Spätmittelalterlichen Ordenswesen*, ed. Elm (Berlin: Duncker and Humblot, 1989), 3–19.

tutional failure. Far from being a period of complete downfall, the late Middle Ages witnessed many calls for reform like Clamanges' within the Church that presaged not Martin Luther and the Protestant Reformation, as Lydius would have it in his 1613 edition of Clamanges' texts, but rather the Council of Trent. In Clamanges' writings, we hear the orthodox calls for reform *in membris* centered around the *reformatio personalis* of the cleric-in-training and ultimately directed toward improvements in the *cura animarum,* as well as the demand for the renewal of episcopal leadership, that were hallmarks of Trent's systematic reform program.

Clamanges' place in the history of reform becomes clear in light of the bonds that existed among patristic reform principles, medieval spirituality, late medieval humanism, and Trent's program. The patristic emphasis on personal renewal repeated in Clamanges' thought was embraced by Trent as the building blocks for the reform of the entire body of the Church a century after his death.[11] Catholic reformers around the time of Trent urged the Church to recapture her core mission through the moral regeneration of the hierarchy (especially diocesan bishops), the parish clergy, and the body of the faithful. This inside-out, *in membris* reform, just like Clamanges', aimed to rejuvenate the Church from within via individual prayer, penitence, asceticism, purgation, and spiritual progress. As John C. Olin concluded with reference to the sixteenth century, "Catholic reform, in short, had a marked personal and pastoral orientation." Spiritual ascent in the fifteenth and sixteenth centuries was especially fostered through ascetic practices and systematic meditative piety, particularly concerning the life of Christ. This spirituality was promoted by Clamanges during the Schism and later championed by, among many others during early modern Catholicism, Ignatius of Loyola and his new Jesuit order.

In their emphasis on the partnership that existed between divine aid and human efforts, humanists including Clamanges directed their atten-

11. The centrality of personal reform in the Fathers was, as noted, one of the major contributions of Ladner's *The Idea of Reform.* For the same theme embedded in Trent's reform program, see the following on which these concluding thoughts rely: Robert E. McNally, "The Council of Trent, the *Spiritual Exercises,* and the Catholic Reform," *Church History* 34 (1965): 36–49; Evenett, *The Spirit of the Counter-Reformation,* 23–42; and Olin, *Catholic Reform,* 1–43 with quotation at 35.

tion to personal reform.[12] Trent's spiritual reform similarly focused on the individual; any institutional or structural reform, most notably the establishment of a seminary system, was a means to promote personal and pastoral reform instead of being an end in itself. Concentrating on the Church *in membris,* Trent's seminaries advocated the moral formation and personal spiritual growth of the prospective pastor under the guardianship of a more watchful and pastorally-oriented episcopacy. As Hubert Jedin assessed the situation, the Protestant Revolution was not the result of falling standards, but was brought on by rising Catholic expectations *in membris* that were not met *in capite.* In order to be successful, head and members had to reform together; since they failed to do so, any steps forward were incomplete and short-lived. Still, the seeds of self-reform had been sown before Luther and were built upon by Trent.[13] There were, indeed, attempts at Tridentine-like personal and pastoral reforms before Luther that came to fruition at the Council of Trent. At the end of the day, Clamanges' spirituality of *reformatio personalis*—especially as it focused on the imitation of Christ as a man of suffering, contemplation, and active service—may be seen as one such bridge over which the Fathers' model of personal reform was passed along from late medieval to early modern Catholicism.

12. John F. D'Amico noted that, "In general, humanist reform thought emphasized personal amelioration rather than institutional change": "Humanism and Pre-Reformation Theology," in *Renaissance Humanism. Foundations, Forms, and Legacy,* 3 vols., ed. Albert Rabil, Jr. (Philadelphia: University of Pennsylvania Press, 1988), 3:366.

13. Hubert Jedin, *Geschichte des Konzils von Trient* (Freiburg: Herder, 1949), 1:111–32.

Select Bibliography

❧

I. Primary Sources

Bérier, François, ed. "Nicolas de Clamanges." Opuscules." 2 vols. Ph.D. diss., École Pratique de Hautes Études, 1974.

Cecchetti, Dario. "'Descriptio loci' e 'Laudatio urbis.'" Persistenza e rinnovamento di strutture retoriche nell'opera di Nicolas de Clamanges." *Annali dell'Istituto Universitario Orientale* 35 (1993): 381–431 with texts at 427–31.

———. "Un egloga inedita di Nicolas de Clamanges." In *Miscellanea di studi e ricerche sul quattrocento francese,* edited by Franco Simone, 25–57 with texts at 49–57. Turin: Giappichelli, 1966.

———, ed. "L'epistolario di Nicolas de Clamanges." Ph.D. diss., Università degli Studi di Torino, 1960.

———. *L'evoluzione del latino umanistico in Francia,* with texts at 96–123, 137–39. Paris: Éditions CEMI, 1986.

———. "Nicolas de Clamanges e Gérard Machet. Contributo allo studio dell' epistolario di Nicolas de Clamanges." *Atti dell'Academia delle scienze di Torino* 100 (1965–66): 133–91 with texts at 183–91.

Coville, Alfred. "Lettres inédites de Nicolas de Clamanges" and "Poésies latines de Nicolas de Clamanges." In *Recherches sur quelques écrivains du XIVe et du XVe siècle,* 253–317. Paris: Droz, 1935.

———. *Le Traité de la ruine de l'Église de Nicholas de Clamanges et la traduction française de 1564.* Paris: Droz, 1936.

Crowder, C. M. D., ed. *Unity, Heresy and Reform 1378–1460: The Conciliar Response to the Great Schism.* London: Edward Arnold, 1977.

d'Achery, Luc, ed. *Spicilegium sive collectio veterum aliquot scriptorum qui in Galliae bibliothecis delituerant,* 1:473–80. Paris, 1655.

Denifle, H., and E. Châtelain, eds. *Chartularium Universitatis Parisiensis.* 4 vols. Paris, 1889–97.

Dupin, Louis Ellies, ed. *Johannis Gersonii . . . Opera Omnia.* 4 vols. Antwerp, 1706.

Fasolt, Constantin, trans. "Nicholas of Clémanges, 'On the Ruin and the Repair of the Church' (ca. 1400)." In *Medieval Europe,* edited by Julius Kirshner and Karl F. Morrison, 434–46. Chicago, Ill.: University of Chicago Press, 1986.

Gerson, Jean. *Oeuvres complètes.* Edited by Palemon Glorieux. 10 vols. Paris: Desclée et Cie, 1960–73.

Leclercq, Jean. "Les prières inédites de Nicolas de Clamanges." *Revue d'ascétique et de mystique* 23 (1947): 171–83.

Lydius, J., ed. *Nicolai de Clemangiis. Opera Omnia.* 3 vols. Leiden, 1613. Reprint in one volume, Farnborough, Hants., England: Gregg Press Limited, 1967.

Tanner, Norman P., ed. *Decrees of the Ecumenical Councils.* 2 vols. London: Sheed and Ward, 1990.

II. Secondary Sources
A. Works concerning Nicolas de Clamanges

Bellitto, Christopher M. "The Rhetoric of Reform: Nicolas de Clamanges' Images of the End." In *Reform and Renewal in the Middle Ages and the Renaissance,* edited by Thomas M. Izbicki and Christopher M. Bellitto, 141–54. Leiden: E. J. Brill, 2000.

Bérier, François. "Exégèse et ironie: À propos de l' *'Expositio super quadraginta septem capitula Ysaye'* de Nicolas de Clamanges (ca. 1425)." *Recherches et travaux. Université de Grenoble Bulletin* 41 (1991): 17–35.

————. "La figure du clerc dans le *'De studio theologico'* de Nicolas de Clamanges." *Travaux de linguistique et de littérature* 21 (1983): 81–103.

————. "L'humaniste, le prêtre et l'enfant mort: le sermon *'De sanctis innocentibus'* de Nicolas de Clamanges." In *L'Enfant au Moyen Âge (littérature et civilisation),* 123–40. Aix-en-Provence: Publications du CUERMA, 1980.

————. "Note sur la datation, la tradition manuscrite et le contenu des dix oraisons de l'humaniste Nicolas de Clamanges." In *La Prière au Moyen Âge (littérature et civilisation),* 7–25. Paris: Champion, 1981.

————. "Remarques sur le *'De lapsu et reparatione iustitiae'* de Nicolas de Clamanges (vers 1360–1437) et sa traduction en français par F. Juret (1553–1626)." *Travaux de littérature* 3 (1990): 25–39.

————. "Remarques sur l'évolution des idées politiques de Nicolas de Clamanges." In *Pratiques de la culture écrite en France au XVe siècle,* edited by Monique Ornato and Nicole Pons, 109–25. Louvain-la-Neuve: Fédération Internationale des Instituts d'Études Médiévales, 1995.

————. "Remarques sur l' *'Expositio super quadraginta septem capitula Isaie'* de Nicolas de Clamanges: Genèse de l'oeuvre, datation, méthode et contenu." In *L'Hostellerie de pensée,* edited by Michel Zink and Danielle Bohler, 41–49. Paris: Presses de l'Université de Paris-Sorbonne, 1995.

Bernstein, Alan E. "Nicholas Poillevillain of Clamanges: A Critical Biography Presented with an Annotated Bibliography of His Published Works." Typescript, Columbia University, 1968.

Cecchetti, Dario. "L'elogio delle arti liberali nel primo umanesimo francese." *Studi Francesi* 28 (1966): 1–14.

————. " *'Florere-deflorescere.'* In margine ad alcuni temi del primo umanesimo francese." In *Mélanges à la mémoire de Franco Simone. France et Italie dans la culture européenne.* Vol. 1, *Moyen Âge et Renaissance,* edited by H. Gaston Hall et al., 143–55. Geneva: Éditions Slatkine, 1980.

———. *Petrarca, Pietramala e Clamanges: storia di una "querelle" inventata.* Paris: Éditions CEMI, 1982.

———. "*'Sic me Cicero laudare docuerat.'* La retorica nel primo umanesimo francese." In *Préludes à la renaissance. Aspects de la vie intellectuelle en France au XVe siècle,* edited by Carla Bozzolo and Ezio Ornato, 47–106. Paris: Édition du CNRS, 1992.

———. "Sulla fortuna del Petrarca in Francia: un testo dimenticato di Nicolas de Clamanges." *Studi Francesi* 31 (1967): 201–22.

———. "La 'Traditio' quintilianea nel quattrocento francese: Gli umanisti francesi precedettero quelli italiani nella riscoperta della 'Institutio Oratoria' integra?" In *L'arte dell'interpretare,* 145–64. Cuneo: Arciere, 1984.

Chesney, Kathleen. "Nicolas de Clamanges: Some Supplementary Biographical Notes." *Medium aevum* 7 (1938): 98–104.

Combes, André. "Sur les 'lettres de consolation' de Nicolas de Clamanges à Pierre d'Ailly." *Archives d'histoire doctrinale et littéraire du Moyen Âge* 13 (1940–42): 359–89.

Coville, Alfred. "Nicolas de Clamanges à l'Index au XVIe siècle." In *Mélanges offerts à M. Abel Lefranc,* 1–16. Paris: Droz, 1936.

Glorieux, Palemon. "Moeurs de la Chrétienté au temps de Jeanne d'Arc: le 'Traité contre l'institution de fêtes nouvelles' de Nicolas de Clamanges." *Mélanges de sciences religieuses* 23 (1966): 15–29.

———. "Notations biographiques sur Nicolas de Clamanges." In *Mélanges offerts à M.-D. Chenu,* ed. André Duval, 291–310. Paris: J. Vrin, 1967.

Hemmerle, Peter. "Nikolaus Poillevillain, gennant Nikolaus von Clemanges und die Schrift, 'De corrupto ecclesiae statu.'" *Historisches Jahrbuch* 27 (1906): 803–12.

Kwanten, A. "Nicolas de Clamanges et l'Imitation de Jésus-Christ." *Mémoires de la société d'agriculture, de commerce, des sciences et arts du départment de la Marne* 74 (1959): 91–100.

Müntz, A. *Nicolas de Clémanges, sa vie et ses écrits.* Strasbourg, 1846.

Ornato, Ezio. "Les humanistes français et le redécouverte des classiques." In *Préludes à la renaissance. Aspects de la vie intellectuelle en France au XVe siècle,* edited by Carla Bozzolo and Ezio Ornato, 1–45. Paris: Édition du CNRS, 1992.

———. *Jean Muret et ses amis, Nicolas de Clamanges et Jean de Montreuil. Contribution à l'étude des rapports entre les humanistes de Paris et ceux d'Avignon (1394–1420).* Geneva: Droz, 1969.

Santoni, Pierre. "Les lettres de Nicolas de Clamanges à Gérard Machet. Un humaniste devant la crise du royaume et de l'Église (1410–1417)." *Mélanges de l'École française de Rome. Moyen Âge temps modernes* 99 (1987): 793–823.

Schuberth, G. *Nicolaus von Clemanges, der Verfasser der Schrift De corrupto ecclesiae statu.* Grossenhaim, 1888.

Simon, Anton. *Studien zur Nikolaus von Clemanges.* Endingen: Druck von Emil Wild, 1929.

B. General

Ampe, Albert. *L'Imitation de Jésus-Christ et son auteur. Réflexions critiques.* Rome: Edizioni di Storia e Letteratura, 1973.

Amundsen, Darrel W. "The Medieval Catholic Tradition." In *Caring and Curing: Health and Medicine in the Western Religious Traditions,* edited by Ronald L. Numbers and Darrel W. Amundsen, 65–107. New York: Macmillan, 1986.

Arbesmann, Rudolph. "The Concept of *Christus medicus* in St. Augustine." *Traditio* 10 (1954): 1–28.

Bellitto, Christopher M. "The Early Development of Pierre d'Ailly's Conciliarism." *Catholic Historical Review* 83 (1997): 217–32.

Benson, Robert L., and Giles Constable, with Carol D. Lanham, eds. *Renaissance and Renewal in the Twelfth Century.* Cambridge: Harvard University Press, 1982.

Bonet-Maury, G. *Gérard Groote, un précurseur de la réforme.* Paris: Librairie Sandoz et Fischbacher, 1878.

Bouwsma, William J. "The Spirituality of Renaissance Humanism." In *Christian Spirituality: High Middle Ages and Reformation,* edited by Jill Raitt, 236–51. New York: Crossroad, 1988.

Boyle, Leonard E. "The Constitution *'Cum ex eo'* of Boniface VIII." *Mediaeval Studies* 24 (1962): 263–302.

———. "The *Oculus Sacerdotis* and Some Other Works of William of Pagula." *Transactions of the Royal Historical Society,* 5th ser., 5 (1955): 81–110.

———. "The *Quodlibets* of St. Thomas and Pastoral Care." *The Thomist* 38 (1974): 232–56.

———. "Robert Grosseteste and the Pastoral Care." *Medieval and Renaissance Studies* 8 (1979): 3–51.

Brandmüller, Walter. *Das Konzil von Konstanz, 1414–1418.* 2 vols. Paderborn: F. Schöningh, 1991–97.

Brown, D. Catherine. *Pastor and Laity in the Theology of Jean Gerson.* Cambridge: Cambridge University Press, 1987.

Burrows, Mark S. *Jean Gerson and De Consolatione Theologiae (1418): The Consolation of a Biblical and Reforming Theology for a Disordered Age.* Tübingen: J. C. B. Mohr (Paul Siebeck), 1991.

Chatelain, Émile. "Les manuscrits du Collège de Navarre en 1741." *Revue des bibliothèques* 11 (1901): 362–411.

Chenu, M.-D. *La théologie au douzième siècle.* Paris: J. Vrin, 1957.

Chiavassa-Gouron, Isabelle. "Les lectures des maîtres et étudiants du collège de Navarre: Un aspect de la vie intellectuelle à l'Université de Paris (1380–1520)." M.A. thesis, École Nationale des Chartes, 1985.

Combes, André. "Gerson et la naissance de l'humanisme." *Revue du Moyen Âge latin* 1 (1945): 259–84.

———. *Jean de Montreuil et le chancelier Gerson.* Paris: J. Vrin, 1942.

Congar, Y.-M. *Vraie et fausse réforme dans l'Église.* 2d ed. Paris: Les Éditions du Cerf, 1968.

Constable, Giles. "The Popularity of Twelfth-Century Spiritual Writers in the Late Middle Ages." In *Renaissance Studies in Honor of Hans Baron,* edited by Anthony Molho and John A. Tedeschi, 5–28. Dekalb, Ill.: Northern Illinois University Press, 1971.

———. *Three Studies in Medieval Religious and Social Thought.* Cambridge: Cambridge University Press, 1995.

———. "Twelfth-Century Spirituality and the Late Middle Ages." *Medieval and Renaissance Studies* 5 (1971): 27–60.

Courtenay, William J. "Spirituality and Late Scholasticism." In *Christian Spirituality: High Middle Ages and Reformation,* edited by Jill Raitt, 109–20. New York: Crossroad, 1988.

Cousins, Ewert. "The Humanity and the Passion of Christ." In *Christian Spirituality: High Middle Ages and Reformation,* edited by Jill Raitt, 375–91. New York: Crossroad, 1988.

Coville, Alfred. *Gontier et Pierre Col et l'humanisme en France au temps de Charles VI.* Paris: Droz, 1934.

———. *La vie intellectuelle dans les domaines d'Avignon-Provence, de 1380 à 1435.* Paris: Droz, 1941.

D'Amico, John F. "Humanism and Pre-Reformation Theology." In *Renaissance Humanism: Foundations, Forms, and Legacy,* edited by Albert Rabil, Jr., 3:349–79. Philadelphia: University of Pennsylvania Press, 1988.

Driver, Steven D. "The Development of Jerome's Views on the Ascetic Life." *Recherches de théologie ancienne et médiévale* 62 (1995): 65–70.

Elm, Kaspar. "Reform- und Observanzbestrebungen im Spätmittelalterlichen Ordenswesen. Ein Überblick." In *Reformbemühungen und Observanzbestrebungen im Spätmittelalterlichen Ordenswesen,* edited by Kaspar Elm, 3–19. Berlin: Duncker and Humblot, 1989.

Evennett, H. O. *The Spirit of the Counter Reformation.* Cambridge: Cambridge University Press, 1968.

Féret, P. *La Faculté de théologie de Paris et ses docteurs les plus célèbres. Moyen Âge.* 4 vols. Paris: Picard, 1897.

Fliche, Augustin, and Victor Martin, eds. *Histoire de l'Église depuis les origines jusqu'à nos jours.* Vol. 14, *L'Église au temps du Grand Schisme et de la crise conciliaire (1378–1449),* by E. Delaruelle, E.-R. LaBande, and Paul Ourliac. Paris: Bloud et Gay, 1962.

Garin, Eugenio. "La '*Dignitas hominis*' e le letteratura patristica." *Rinascita* 4 (1938): 102–46.

Gill, Joseph. "The Fifth Session of the Council of Constance." *Heythrop Journal* 5 (1964): 131–43.

Gorochov, Nathalie. *Le Collège de Navarre de sa fondation (1305) au début du XVe siècle (1418).* Paris: Champion, 1997.

Gründler, Otto. *"Devotio Moderna."* In *Christian Spirituality: High Middle Ages and Reformation,* edited by Jill Raitt, 375–91. New York: Crossroad, 1988.

———. *"Devotio Moderna Atque Antiqua:* The Modern Devotion and Carthusian Spirituality." In *The Spirituality of Western Christendom.* Vol. 2, *The Roots of the Modern Christian Tradition,* edited by E. Rozanne Elder, 27–45. Kalamazoo, Mich.: Cistercian Publications, 1984.

Guenée, Bernard. *Between Church and State: The Lives of Four French Prelates in the Late Middle Ages.* Translated by Arthur Goldhammer. Chicago: University of Chicago Press, 1991.

Helmrath, Johannes. "Reform als Thema der Konzilien des Spätmittelalters." In *Christian Unity: The Council of Ferrara-Florence 1438/9–1989,* edited by Giuseppe Alberigo, 75–152. Leuven: Leuven University Press, 1991.

———. "Theorie und Praxis der Kirchenreform im Spätmittelalter." *Rottenburger Jahrbuch für Kirchengeschichte* 11 (1992): 41–70.

Hundersmarck, Lawrence F. "Preaching the Passion: Late Medieval 'Lives of Christ' as Sermon Vehicles." In *De Ore Domini: Preacher and Word in the Middle Ages,* edited by Thomas L. Amos, Eugene A. Green, and Beverly Mayne Kienzle, 147–67. Kalamazoo, Mich.: Medieval Institute Publications, 1989.

———. "A Study of the Spiritual Themes in the Prayers and Passion Narration of Ludolphus de Saxonia's *Vita Jesu Christi.*" Ph.D. diss., Fordham University, 1983.

Jacob, E. F. "Christian Humanism." In *Europe in the Late Middle Ages,* edited by J. R. Hale et al., 437–65. Evanston, Ill.: Northwestern University Press, 1965.

———. *Essays in the Conciliar Epoch.* 2d ed. Manchester: Manchester University Press, 1953.

Jedin, Hubert. *Geschichte des Konzils von Trient.* Vol. 1. Freiburg: Herder, 1949.

Jullien de Pommerol, Marie-Henriette, and Jacques Monfrin. *La bibliothèque pontificale à Avignon et à Peniscola pendant le Grand Schisme d'Occident et sa dispersion. Inventaires et concordances.* Rome: École Française de Rome, 1991.

Kaminsky, Howard. "The Early Career of Simon de Cramaud." *Speculum* 49 (1974): 499–534.

———. *Simon de Cramaud and the Great Schism.* New Brunswick, N.J.: Rutgers University Press, 1983.

Kieckhefer, Richard. "Major Currents in Late Medieval Devotion." In *Christian Spirituality: High Middle Ages and Reformation,* edited by Jill Raitt, 75–108. New York: Crossroad, 1988.

Kristeller, Paul Oskar. *Renaissance Thought and Its Sources.* Edited by Michael Moony. New York: Columbia University Press, 1979.

Ladner, Gerhart B. *The Idea of Reform: Its Impact on Christian Thought and Action in the Age of the Fathers.* Cambridge: Harvard University Press, 1959. Reprint, New York: Harper & Row, 1967.

———. *Images and Ideas in the Middle Ages.* 2 vols. Rome: Edizioni di Storia e Letteratura, 1983.

———. *"Reformatio."* In *Ecumenical Dialogue at Harvard,* edited by Samuel H. Miller and G. E. Wright, 172–90. Cambridge: Harvard University Press, 1964.

———. "Terms and Ideas of Renewal." In *Renaissance and Renewal in the Twelfth Century,* edited by Robert L. Benson and Giles Constable with Carol D. Landham, 1–33. Cambridge: Harvard University Press, 1982.

———. "Vegetation Symbolism and the Concept of Renaissance." In *De artibus opuscula XL: Essays in Honor of Erwin Panofsky,* edited by Millard Meiss, 303–22. New York: New York University Press, 1961.

Lecler, Joseph. "Le cardinalat de l'Église romaine: son évolution dans l'histoire." *Études* 330 (1969): 871–79.

———. *"Pars corporis papae*—le Sacré Collège dans l'ecclésiologie medievale." In *L'homme devant Dieu: Mélanges offerts au Père Henri de Lubac,* 2:183–98. Paris: Aubier, 1964.

Leff, Gordon. *Paris and Oxford Universities in the Thirteenth and Fourteenth Centuries.* New York: John Wiley and Sons, 1968.

Mayeur, Jean-Marie et al., eds. *Histoire du Christianisme des origines à nos jours.* Vol. 6, *Un temp d'épreuves (1274–1449),* edited by Michel Mollat du Jourdin et André Vauchez. Paris: Desclée-Fayard, 1990.

McNally, Robert E. "The Council of Trent, the *Spiritual Exercises* and the Catholic Reform." *Church History* 34 (1965): 36–49.

———. "Pope Adrian VI (1522–23) and Church Reform." *Archivum historiae pontificiae* 7 (1969): 253–85.

———. *Reform of the Church.* New York: Herder and Herder, 1963.

———. *The Unreformed Church.* New York: Sheed and Ward, 1965.

Miethke, Jürgen. "Kirchenreform auf den Konzilien des 15. Jahrhunderts. Motive-Methoden-Wirkungen." In *Studien zum 15. Jahrhundert,* 2 vols., edited by Johannes Helmrath and Heribert Müller, 1:13–42. Munich: Oldenbourg, 1994.

Millet, Hélène. "Du conseil au concile (1395–1408). Recherche sur le nature des assemblées du clergé en France pendant le Grand Schisme d'Occident." *Journal des savants* (1985): 137–59.

Millet, Hélène, and Emmanuel Poulle. *Le vote de la soustraction d'obédience en 1398, I: Introduction. Édition et facsimilés des bulletins du vote.* Paris: Édition du CNRS, 1988.

Minnich, Nelson H. "Concepts of Reform Proposed at the Fifth Lateran Council." *Archivum historiae pontificiae* 7 (1969): 163–251.

Mollat, G. *The Popes at Avignon.* 9th ed. Translated by Janet Love. New York: Harper & Row, 1965.

Oakley, Francis. *The Political Thought of Pierre d'Ailly: The Voluntarist Tradition.* New Haven: Yale University Press, 1964.

———. *The Western Church in the Later Middle Ages.* Ithaca: Cornell University Press, 1979.

Oberman, Heiko A. *The Dawn of the Reformation.* Edinburgh: T. & T. Clark, 1986.

———. *Forerunners of the Reformation.* New York: Holt, Rinehart and Winston, 1966.

———. *Masters of the Reformation: The Emergence of a New Intellectual Climate in Europe.* Cambridge: Cambridge University Press, 1981.

Olin, John C., ed. *Catholic Reform: From Cardinal Ximenes to the Council of Trent 1495–1563.* New York: Fordham University Press, 1990.

O'Malley, John W. *Giles of Viterbo on Church and Reform: A Study in Renaissance Thought.* Leiden: E. J. Brill, 1968.

———. "Historical Thought and the Reform Crisis of the Early Sixteenth Century." *Theological Studies* 28 (1967): 531–48.

———. *Praise and Blame in Renaissance Rome: Rhetoric, Doctrine and Reform in the Sacred Orators of the Papal Court, c. 1450–1521.* Durham, N.C.: Duke University Press, 1979.

———. "Reform, Historical Consciousness, and Vatican II's *Aggiornamento*." *Theological Studies* 32 (1971): 573–601.

Ouy, Gilbert. "Le collège de Navarre, berceau de l'humanisme français." *Actes du 95e congrès national des sociétés savantes, Reims 1970. Section de philologie et d'histoire jusqu'à 1610.* Vol. 1, *Enseignement et vie intellectuelle (IXe–XVIe siècle)*, 275–99. Paris: Bibliothèque Nationale, 1975.

———. "Gerson et l'Angleterre." In *Humanism in France at the End of the Middle Ages and in the Early Renaissance,* edited by A. H. T. Levi, 45–49. Manchester: Manchester University Press, 1970.

———. "L'humanisme et les mutations politiques et sociales en France au XIVe et XVe siècles." In *L'humanisme français au début de la Renaissance,* 27–44. Paris: J. Vrin, 1973.

———. "In Search of the Earliest Traces of French Humanism: The Evidence from Codicology." *Library Chronicle* 43 (1978): 3–38.

———. "Paris, l'un des principaux foyers de l'humanisme en Europe au début du XVe siècle." *Bulletin de la société de l'histoire de Paris et de l'Île-de-France* (1967–68): 71–98.

———. "Le thème du *'Taedium scriptorum gentilium'* chez les humanistes, particulièrement en France au début du XVe siècle." *Cahiers de l'association internationale des études françaises* 23 (1971): 9–26.

Ozment, Steven. *The Age of Reform 1250–1550: An Intellectual and Religious History of Late Medieval and Reformation Europe.* New Haven: Yale University Press, 1980.

———. "The University and the Church: Patterns of Reform in Jean Gerson." *Medievalia et Humanistica,* n.s., 1 (1970): 111–26.

Pascoe, Louis B. "Jean Gerson: The *Ecclesia primitiva* and Reform." *Traditio* 30 (1974): 379–409.

———. "Jean Gerson: Mysticism, Conciliarism, and Reform." *Annuarium historiae conciliorum* 6 (1974): 135–53.

————. *Jean Gerson: Principles of Church Reform*. Leiden: E. J. Brill, 1973.

————. "Theological Dimensions of Pierre d'Ailly's Teachings on Papal Plenitude of Power." *Annuarium historiae conciliorum* 11 (1979): 357–66.

Pelikan, Jaroslav. *Reformation of Church and Dogma 1300–1700*. Chicago: University of Chicago Press, 1984.

Post, R. R. *The Modern Devotion*. Leiden: E. J. Brill, 1968.

Rice, Eugene F., Jr. "Humanism in France." In *Renaissance Humanism: Foundations, Forms, and Legacy*, edited by Albert Rabil, Jr., 2:109–22. Philadelphia: University of Pennsylvania Press, 1988.

Roccati, G. Matteo. "La formation des humanistes dans le dernier quart du XIVe siècle." In *Pratiques de la culture écrite en France au XVe siècle*, edited by Monique Ornato and Nicole Pons, 55–73. Louvain-la-Neuve: Fédération Internationale des Instituts d'Études Médiévales, 1995.

————. "La formazione intellettuale di Jean Gerson (1363–1429): Un esempio del rinnovamento umanistico degli studi." In *L'educazione e la formazione intellettuale nell'età dell'umanesimo*, edited by Luisa Rotondi Secchi Tarugi, 229–44. Milan: Guerini e Associati, 1992.

Rummel, Erika. *The Humanist-Scholastic Debate in the Renaissance and Reformation*. Cambridge: Harvard University Press, 1995.

Southern, R. W. *Medieval Humanism and Other Studies*. Oxford: Basil Blackwell, 1970.

————. *Scholastic Humanism and the Unification of Europe*. Vol. 1, *Foundations*. Oxford: Basil Blackwell, 1995.

Stump, Phillip H. *The Reforms of the Council of Constance (1414–1418)*. Leiden: E. J. Brill, 1994.

Swanson, R. N. *Religion and Devotion in Europe, c. 1215–c. 1515*. Cambridge: Cambridge University Press, 1995.

————. *Universities, Academics and the Great Schism*. Cambridge: Cambridge University Press, 1979.

Tierney, Brian. "A Conciliar Theory of the Thirteenth Century." *Catholic Historical Review* 36 (1951): 415–40.

————. *Foundations of the Conciliar Theory*. Cambridge: Cambridge University Press, 1955.

————. "Hermeneutics and History: The Problem of *Haec Sancta*." In *Essays in Medieval History Presented to Bertie Wilkinson*, edited by T. A. Sandquist and F. M. Powicke, 354–70. Toronto: University of Toronto Press, 1969.

————. "Hostiensis and Collegiality." In *Proceedings of the Fourth International Congress of Medieval Canon Law*, edited by Stephan Kuttner, 401–9. Vatican City: Biblioteca Apostolica Vaticana, 1976.

Trinkaus, Charles. *In Our Image and Likeness: Humanity and Divinity in Italian Humanist Thought*. 2 vols. Chicago: University of Chicago Press, 1970.

————. "Italian Humanism and Scholastic Theology." In *Renaissance Humanism: Foundations, Forms, and Legacy*, edited by Albert Rabil, Jr., 3:327–48. Philadelphia: University of Pennsylvania Press, 1988.

Ullmann, Walter. *Origins of the Great Schism*. London: Methuen, 1948.

Valois, Noël. *La France et le Grand Schisme d'Occident*. 4 vols. Paris, 1896–1902.

Van Engen, John, trans. *Devotio Moderna: Basic Writings*. New York: Paulist Press, 1988.

————. "Images and Ideas: The Achievements of Gerhart Burian Ladner, with a Bibliography of His Published Works." *Viator* 20 (1989): 85–115.

————. "Late Medieval Anticlericalism: The Case of the New Devout." In *Anticlericalism in Late Medieval and Early Modern Europe*, edited by Peter A. Dykema and Heiko A. Oberman, 19–52. Leiden: E. J. Brill, 1993.

————. *Rupert of Deutz*. Berkeley: University of California Press, 1983.

Vasoli, Cesare. "Les débuts de l'humanisme a l'université de Paris." In *Preuve et raisons a l'université de Paris. Logique, ontologie et théologie au XIVe siècle*, edited by Zenon Kaluza and Paul Vignaux, 269–86. Paris: J. Vrin, 1984.

Verger, Jacques. "The University of Paris at the End of the Hundred Years' War." In *Universities in Politics: Case Studies from the Late Middle Ages and Early Modern Period*, edited by John W. Baldwin and Richard A. Goldthwaite, 47–78. Baltimore: Johns Hopkins University Press, 1972.

Witt, Ronald G. "Medieval Italian Culture and the Origins of Humanism as a Stylistic Ideal." In *Renaissance Humanism: Foundations, Forms, and Legacy*, edited by Albert Rabil, Jr., 1:29–70. Philadelphia: University of Pennsylvania Press, 1988.

Index

*Nicolas de Clamanges: Spirituality, Personal Reform, and Pastoral Renewal on the
Eve of the Reformations* was designed and composed in Adobe Garamond
with Centaur display by Kachergis Book Design, Pittsboro,
North Carolina, and printed on 60-pound Writers Offset Natural
and bound by Thomson-Shore, Dexter, Michigan.

DATE DUE

Demco, Inc 38-293